Buying & Selling Jewelry on eBay®

Stacey King Gordon

THOMSON
TM
COURSE TECHNOLOGY
Professional ■ Trade ■ Reference

ISBN: 1-59200-609-4

Library of Congress Catalog Card Number: 2004114491

Printed in the United States of America

05 06 07 08 09 BH 10 9 8 7 6 5 4 3 2 1

THOMSON

COURSE TECHNOLOGY ™

Professional ■ Trade ■ Reference

Thomson Course Technology PTR,
a division of Thomson Course Technology
25 Thomson Place
Boston, MA 02210
http://www.courseptr.com

**Publisher and GM of
Course Technology PTR:**
Stacy L. Hiquet

Associate Director of Marketing:
Sarah O'Donnell

Marketing Managers:
Heather Hurley and
Kristin Eisenzopf

Manager of Editorial Services:
Heather Talbot

Associate Acquisitions Editor:
Megan Belanger

Senior Editor:
Mark Garvey

Marketing Coordinator:
Jordan Casey

Developmental Editor:
Kate Shoup Welsh

Technical Reviewer:
Morgan Beard

**PTR Editorial Services
Coordinator:**
Elizabeth Furbish

Interior Layout Tech:
Shawn Morningstar

Cover Designer:
Laura Rickenbach

Indexer:
Katherine Stimson

Proofreader:
Cindy Fields

To Andrew, for everything

Acknowledgments

Many special thanks to everyone who contributed to the writing of this book: my supportive and insightful editors Megan Belanger, Kate Shoup Welsh, and Morgan Beard; Ann Poletti, Sravanthi Agrawal, and Shannon Stubo at eBay; and Peggy Jo Donahue at *Professional Jeweler*. Also, many thanks to the enthusiastic eBayers who shared their stories with me.

About the Author

STACEY KING GORDON is a writer and editor in the San Francisco Bay Area. A former editor for *Professional Jeweler* and *JCK*, two leading jewelry industry trade magazines, she has also written extensively on topics such as small business and retail, healthcare, finance, and graphic design. She is the author of two design books, *Magazine Design That Works* and *Packaging: Graphic Makeovers for Market Change*.

Contents

Introduction

The eBay Jewelry Adventure

The world of jewelry is one of intrigue. How many other kinds of consumer products have so many exotic and thrilling stories, or at least *possibilities* of stories, surrounding them? The rubies in a ring could have been discovered at the end of a weeks-long trek through a dusty and politically volatile country. An adventurer could have happened upon the perfect emerald in a remote region that the rest of the world had long forgotten about, opening up new hope for the people who make their homes there. More than the simple monetary value of the pieces themselves, it's this aura of romance and daring that actually makes jewelry and gemstones as treasured as they are in our society.

But since you're reading this book, you probably already know that the same mystery surrounding these jewels makes buying and selling them confounding. Gemstones and precious metals can be confusing, with all the characteristics, science, and trade secrets that go into perfecting and marketing them. Even despite attempts to simplify diamond buying with guidelines such as the 4Cs (see the following note) aimed at timid suitors shopping for engagement rings, jewelry can be intimidating for intrepid shoppers. And breaking into the selling game is even tougher in an industry that's been dominated by family businesses for generations.

Note

Diamond sellers use the 4Cs—carat weight, clarity, color, and cut—to grade diamonds and easily educate consumers about them. However, it's harder to find such a straightforward formula for buying and selling other kinds of jewelry, such as colored stones or precious metals.

For decades, independent jewelry stores were the primary outlets where a consumer could buy jewelry. This was not entirely surprising, because in the early and mid 20th century, "mom and pop" shops dominated most retail sales in communities, from groceries and shoe shops to appliance stores and booksellers. The family jeweler served a husband and wife through all their milestones in life, with bridal jewelry and baby charms, anniversary rings and special gifts that commemorated a rise in income and status. Indeed, one of the exciting things about the jewelry industry is that, even as mom and pop shops went by the wayside in other retail categories, surrendering to domineering retail chains, independent retail jewelers held their ground. Independent jewelers still play a major role in selling jewelry today, a sign that consumers want to buy something unique and valuable, like jewelry, from somebody they know and trust.

In the late 1980s, however, retail jewelry stores, like the grocers, shoe shops, appliance stores, and booksellers before them, began to feel the heat of other sales channels. First, mall jewelry stores with enormous advertising budgets sprung up nationwide, and then mass merchandise discount stores such as Wal-Mart and Costco decided to get in the jewelry game. When the Home Shopping Network and QVC began enjoying such incredible success with their jewelry sales, the industry began to get a whiff of the winds of change. Much to everybody's surprise, it became increasingly apparent that consumers were not only seeking competitive bargains, but that they also were starting to become comfortable with buying jewelry they hadn't seen, touched, or held.

How eBay Changed the Landscape

When the Internet took off in the mid-1990s, it shouldn't have been much of a surprise that e-commerce sites would latch on to the idea of selling jewelry online. Nevertheless, many jewelry-industry veterans said it wouldn't last. Especially in the early days, they cited the trust issue. How did you know what you were getting and from whom you were getting it? At least with a home shopping TV network, you had a real, known company backing up the promise. The vets also stood behind their belief that it was impossible to sell a beautiful item like jewelry using a tiny, low-quality image and some text on a page.

But what the naysayers didn't account for was what the Internet *would* provide consumers that was hard to come by before: education. Jewelry buyers could now access information about gemstone cut dimensions, gold stamping, and most controversially, diamond price lists, which detail wholesale pricing much like *The Blue Book* does for automobiles. With education came confidence, and in 10 years or so, U.S. jewelry sales on the Internet grew to about $2.8 billion in 2003—a figure that's predicted to balloon to $8 billion by 2008, according to Forrester Research.

The popularity of eBay influenced this trend profoundly. Back when eBay was in its infancy, a community of avid watch collectors latched on to the online auction format, using eBay to trade very high-end collectibles. According to eBay Jewelry & Watches category manager Ann Poletti, this phenomenon surprised eBay at first, especially because many of the sellers on the site to that point had been trading items such as old computer equipment, toys they'd played with as kids, and similar yard-sale finds. But watch trading grew quickly, as did sales numbers. eBay created Watches as the fifth official category on the site, and it is now one of the largest, if not *the* largest, online watch marketplaces in the world, where one-of-a-kind pieces are traded for prices that regularly exceed $10,000.

Watches paved the way not only for other higher-value merchandise categories, but for antique and estate jewelry collectors and, over time, new jewelry and watches as well. For sellers, the auction site became a way to move old merchandise or to market a business outside of geographic boundaries. For buyers, it was a way to get a good deal and massive selection without having to shop around at a lot of different stores.

Today, jewelry is one of eBay's biggest businesses, with

- 790,000 jewelry and watch auctions at any given time

- $1.3 billion in jewelry and watches sold every year

- 6,000 bids per hour in the Jewelry & Watches category

Despite the fact that eBay is somewhat of a free-for-all, it has become such a strong brand and an established entity that people feel comfortable shopping there. A study in 2004 showed that eBay was the most trusted e-commerce site around, beating out heavy-hitters with e-commerce capacity such as Amazon.com, Hewlett-Packard, IBM, and Procter & Gamble.

Indeed, the loyalty and trust that eBay has built in a very short time is evident in the number of high-ticket pieces that sell every day on the site. In 2003, according to eBay, the most expensive jewelry sale was that of a radiant-cut solitaire diamond ring for $26,459. That same year, a new Audemars Piguet Royal Oak Titanium watch sold for $26,080. Those are the kinds of sales that even jewelry store owners covet.

Why Use Online Auctions?

When I covered the jewelry industry as a journalist, my favorite events of the year were the Magnificent Jewelry auctions at Sotheby's and Christies in New York. The city's most affluent would crowd into the room along with diamond dealers curious to see what price an emerald and diamond necklace being sold by an Arab sheik, or a sapphire ring that once belonged to the Duchess of Windsor's second cousin, would fetch. Inevitably, a mystery caller would swoop in at the last minute to bid by phone on the multimillion dollar piece, only to be countered by some infamous jeweler extraordinaire who had stealthily sneaked in the back door while the bidding was underway.

Online auctions bring that same excitement and thirst for blood home to us "common folk"—except that the items we're bidding on are probably $500 tennis bracelets rather than a $3.5 million yellow diamond tiara. The power of the Internet means that more people can get in the game than ever, which makes things very interesting. But the main reason people turn to eBay is that, whether you're a buyer or a seller, you can always see the prospect of a deal. Sellers get access to hundreds, even thousands, of potential buyers from around the country or around the world, who are usually there because they have money to spend. These sellers can sit back and let the laws of supply and demand work naturally on their behalf—if the piece is fabulous, the price will be right. Buyers also benefit from this system. In many cases, the price for an item is solely driven by the demand for that item at the time that it's being sold—meaning that if other buyers aren't paying close enough attention, you could score a luxury watch or a beautiful diamond for much less than you'd pay in a retail jewelry store.

Note

When it comes to how lucrative eBay can be, the numbers don't lie: As of this writing there were 95 million registered users, with 41 million actively using the site regularly.

It seems like everybody has a story about somebody who quit her job to sell collectibles on eBay, some lucky entrepreneur who's already made her first million. At the same time, everybody has heard the rumors and read the newspaper reports about the rip-offs—the item that never arrived, the knockoff art for which they paid too much, or, especially recently, the scam artists that use eBay to "phish" for credit-card numbers.

So with all these myths and legends, it can be understandably intimidating to get started on eBay. Before you begin as a buyer or seller, my single piece of advice is to move slowly. Do your research, learn how eBay works, and consider your options carefully before committing to anything. Even more importantly, get a feel for what's involved with shopping for and selling jewelry before trying to buy or sell anything. With a little education and planning, you're much more likely to come away as a fully satisfied eBay customer.

Who This Book Is For

If you love jewelry—whether you simply admire the beauty and craft of jewelry or are an experienced industry professional—this book is for you. I've included in these pages a primer on understanding jewelry and how to buy it, but I've also concentrated on how to take an established, bricks-and-mortar jewelry business to the next level using the online auction model. Depending on your level of experience, you might find the sections detailing the science, technology, and handling of jewelry, watches, and gemstones most helpful. Or, if you're already an expert in that area, you might concentrate on how to promote yourself on eBay, establish a lucrative auction business, and navigate the potential pitfalls of dealing with customers in an online setting.

What You'll Find in This Book

This book will step you through the process of becoming a full-fledged jewelry buyer and seller—including finding the perfect gem and the right jewelry style, and understanding the rules of advertising and selling jewelry to consumers. The book will also help you gain confidence in eBay as a marketplace, helping you believe eBay's stance that "people are basically good" —and teaching you to look out for the ones who aren't.

How This Book Is Organized

You don't need to read this whole book before you get started. I encourage you to jump in and get your feet wet. Chapter 1, "Getting Started on eBay," will walk you through the basics of registering for an account and getting to know the landscape. You can even go ahead and bid on a few things just to develop your rhythm. But before you start getting serious, I recommend that you learn about what you're bidding on and selling, which this book will help you do. Next, the book delves into what you should look for as you shop for jewelry and watches on eBay. Chapter 4, "The Ins and Outs of Jewelry Buying," for example, details the characteristics of quality you should look for and common red flags you'll find as you browse eBay categories. Just as important, in later chapters you'll learn how to familiarize with your seller's background, watch out for common scams, and strategize to win an item you really want.

Part 3 of the book is for sellers, and covers how to transition from buying to selling on eBay, and how to find success in a competitive marketplace. Chapter 10, "eBay for the Jewelry Professional," provides insight to established industry members on how they can use eBay to supplement and grow their business, who's buying jewelry on eBay, and how to balance time between eBay and their regular business. Chapter 11, "Creating Compelling —and Legally Correct—Product Descriptions," covers the art of writing descriptions that sell while still accurately and fairly representing an item. Other chapters offer tricks for working out disputes with buyers, shipping jewelry safely, and cutting the corporate cord to become a full-time eBay seller.

So without further ado, let's get you started on eBay by making you an official community member, and introduce you to the wonderful extravaganza that is the eBay jewelry marketplace.

part 1

Deals and Profits on eBay

chapter 1

Getting Started on eBay

If you've never visited eBay before, the first thing that will strike you is how magnificent it is. Like when visiting a major world metropolis for the first time, you'll find yourself thrilled, flabbergasted, and a little overwhelmed by the sheer number of things to see on eBay. Not surprisingly, the first thing you're going to want to do is stroll through the streets of this brilliant new world and just explore.

Before that, however, you need a passport so you can gain access to parts of this place that you won't get to see otherwise. To get started using eBay, simply type **www.ebay.com** in the address bar of Internet Explorer, Netscape Navigator, or whatever Web browser you use. Doing so displays eBay's Welcome page, which contains three columns: Find, Buy, and Pay, as shown in Figure 1.1. From here, in addition to reading up on the bidding and Buy It Now processes, as well as on what payment options are available, you can type a keyword in the search bar or choose from a pull-down menu of 30-odd main categories to explore the site.

My advice? Indulge yourself by spending an hour or two wandering around this extravagant bazaar, the likes of which you've probably never seen. Check out the wacky, the rare, the unbelievably over-the-top items for sale. It's better to get it out of your system *before* you register and are armed with a payment account.

Don't just browse the jewelry. Instead, do some window shopping in the other categories—everything from stamps and toys to automobiles and real estate. Categories and subcategories are scrupulously organized and detailed.

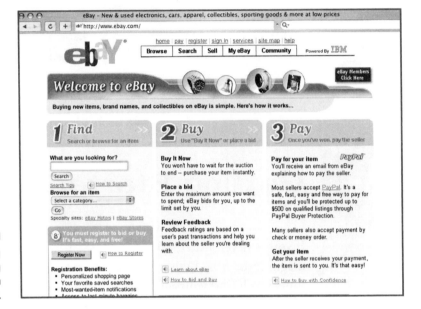

Figure 1.1

eBay simplifies browsing
and buying by grouping
functionality into three main
areas: Find, Buy, and Pay.

Here's an example of how you can browse for exactly what you're looking for:

1. Click on a main category name, such as Consumer Electronics.

2. Click on a subcategory name. If you select CD Players & Recorders, for example, you'll see a listing of a few thousand items on the right side of the screen.

3. Drill down farther by selecting another subcategory, such as Single Disc Players, which has several hundred listings.

4. From here, you can narrow your results by brand—Sony or Bose, for example. This process of elimination helps you locate exactly what you're looking for.

"Hey," you're thinking. "I'm here for jewelry. Why bother looking at the rest?" Simple. Not only will taking this time to explore eBay help prevent you from springing for the first piece you find, it will also give you a feel for just how big eBay's universe is, and how many people are transacting business here.

Setting Goals for Yourself

Good. You got that out of your system. Now, before you proceed, it's important to set objectives for your experience here. Otherwise, you could very likely get carried away, impulsively bidding on something you have no use for, or listing your good silverware just to see what you'll get for it.

Goals for Buyers

Before you start shopping in earnest, take a moment to ask yourself a few questions, and keep your answers firm in your mind:

- Are you looking for one kind of item in particular? If so, what are its characteristics? Are you looking for a specific designer or brand? A definite carat weight, color, or cut?

- Do you want something new, or are you looking for something pre-owned? Do you want something from a particular era, or at least something in the *style* of that era?

- What kind of condition are you willing to settle for?

- Is this a one-time buy, or are you adding to or starting a collection?

- For whom are you buying the item?

- How much do you know about the item you want to buy?

These questions might seem unnecessarily limiting. After all, you're shopping! Where's the fun in interrogating yourself about what you want before you see what the possibilities are? But in truth, these are the same questions you should ask yourself if you're going to buy jewelry or a watch from the reputable jewelry store downtown, the pawn shop in the strip mall on the edge of town, or the friend of your co-worker's who deals out of an upstairs office in the diamond district.

Jewelry is an emotional purchase. It's easy to get carried away by the sparkle of a stone, the pedigree of an antique piece, or the anticipation of the joy on the recipient's face when she opens the box. That's why it's important to use your head, especially when you're ready to start bidding.

Goals for Sellers

If you're selling rather than buying, then again, a firm set of guidelines will help you get what you want from your experience. Ask yourself the following:

- Is this a one-time sale, or are you hoping to continue selling jewelry on eBay in the future?

- How much do you know about the piece you're selling?

- How experienced are you with jewelry in general?

- How much money do you need to make selling this item to ensure you turn an acceptable profit?

- How much time are you willing and able to put into this sale to make it worthwhile for you?

Answering these questions can help you with the logistics of a successful auction: writing a description, deciding on reserves or starting prices, and establishing shipping and payment policies that work within your time limitations. But it will also help you pave the way for a future on eBay. Your goals will let you decide how to promote yourself and your business early in the game, develop an attitude toward dealing with your customers, and more selectively choose the products you hope to sell.

Registering for eBay

After you've gotten to know your way around the site a little, it's time to register. Before you do, however, you should firmly understand the following site rules and regulations:

- **You must be 18 or older to use the site.** Only people who are permitted to form legally binding contracts may participate in eBay transactions.

- **A bid is a contract.** If you bid on an item and win it, it's yours, and you must pay for it. You can't retract a bid after you submit it, except in exceptional circumstances (see Chapter 6, "When, and How, to Bid," for more details).

- **Don't blame eBay.** eBay makes clear in its user agreement that it is not an "auctioneer," but rather an online meeting place for buyers and sellers. Although the company will provide some recourse for dealing with fraudulent sellers, eBay itself is *not* responsible for getting your money back if you lose it.

- **eBay protects your privacy.** eBay won't sell your information to marketers. That said, when you sign up on eBay, you might still want to provide an e-mail account on which you don't mind getting a lot of spam, because once your user ID is posted for the world to see, you'll probably start receiving more unsolicited e-mail.

Stepping Through eBay's Registration Process

Regardless of whether you plan to buy or sell on eBay, you must first register with the site. Registering on eBay is simple. Just do the following:

Note

The process outlined here gets you set up as a buyer; sellers will need to take additional steps, which are outlined momentarily.

1. Click the Register Now button under Find (refer to Figure 1.1).

2. eBay displays its Registration screen, as shown in Figure 1.2. Type your first and last name in the fields provided.

3. Enter your street address, city, state, ZIP or postal code, and country.

4. Type your primary telephone number (and, optionally, a secondary number).

5. Enter your e-mail address in both the Email address and the Re-enter email address fields to ensure that you've typed it correctly.

6. In the Create your eBay User ID field, type the name, or handle, you want to use on the site. If the first few names you try are already taken, keep trying; just make sure the ID you choose is both distinctive and anonymous. (That is, don't use your full name or your e-mail address.)

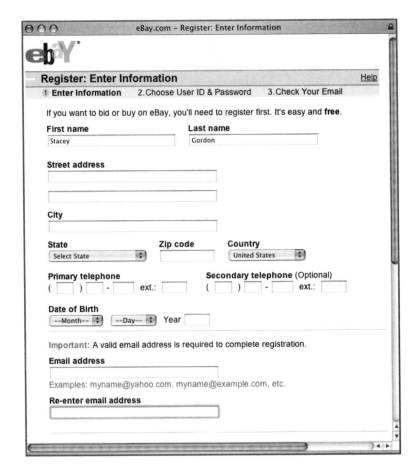

Figure 1.2

By providing some basic information about yourself, you'll be up and running with an eBay buyer's account in a matter of minutes.

Note

Over time, your user ID will become your badge of honor in the eBay marketplace. Even though you technically remain anonymous on the site, your user ID and all the information associated with it tells sellers and other bidders everything they need to know about doing business with and bidding against you.

7. Choose a password that's easy to remember, but not easy to guess. To ensure that the password you enter is correct, you'll need to type it twice—once in the Create password field, and a second time in the Re-enter password field.

8. In the Secret question drop-down list, choose a question for eBay to use to verify your ID in the event you forget your user name and/or password. Then, in the Secret answer field, type the answer to the question.

9. Enter your date of birth in the fields provided.

10. Click Continue.

11. eBay displays its user agreement and privacy policy (see Figure 1.3). Read it over (be sure to scroll down in both windows to read both agreements in full), click the I am 18+ years old and the I understand that I can choose not to receive communications from eBay check boxes to select them, and then click the I Agree to These Terms button.

12. eBay will automatically send you an e-mail message to verify that the e-mail address you entered is correct. When you receive the message, click the Complete eBay Registration button in the body of the e-mail. Doing so completes the registration process and returns you to eBay's Web site. Smile, you're on eBay!

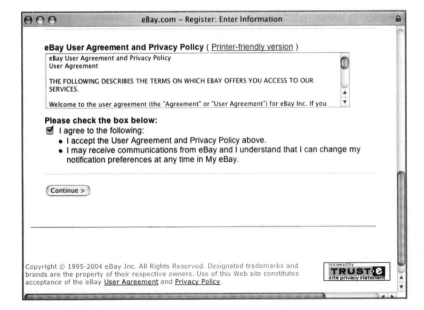

Figure 1.3

eBay requires that you read and agree to its user agreement and privacy policy before completing the buyer registration process.

Tip

Spending time as a buyer will allow you to chalk up some feedback from other eBay members, which you'll want to do before you try to sell anything on the site. In the eBay community, sellers who don't have feedback are regarded with suspicion. See Chapter 7, "What Happens if You Win," and Chapter 12, "Sealing the Deal," for more on giving and receiving feedback.

Setting Up a Seller's Account

Once you have completed your eBay registration, you are welcome to establish a seller's account using your eBay user ID and password. You don't necessarily need to have something to sell to set up an account; you might just want to have one established in case you want to get started quickly when you do have a piece to offload.

Sellers have an additional set of rules by which they need to abide:

- **Your listing must be legal and relevant.** You must be legally allowed to sell the item you're listing, you're obligated to list it in the appropriate category, and any content or images you provide must be directly relevant to what you're actually selling.

- **Fork over the goods.** If you receive at least one bid for your item, you are required to sell the item to the highest bidder—even if you don't net the amount you were hoping for. The only exceptions are if you don't receive payment from the bidder, you can't confirm the buyer's identity, or you've set a reserve price that was not met by the bids tendered (see Chapter 9, "From Buyer to Seller," for more details on reserve prices).

- **Fraud doesn't pay.** If eBay has concrete evidence that you have conducted any fraudulent activity on the site, the company can suspend or terminate your account.

- **Thou shall not shill.** You absolutely cannot in any way manipulate the price of the item you're selling. Known as "shilling," this practice usually involves sellers who log on as different users and bid on their item to drive the price up. This is a huge no-no, and can result in account termination.

To establish a seller's account, do the following:

1. Log in to eBay using your new user ID and password.

2. On the top navigation bar, click Sell.

3. On the page that appears, click the Sell Your Item button (see Figure 1.4).

4. If you are not yet logged in, you will see a page prompting you to log in using your eBay user ID and password. Once you're logged in, the Seller's Account registration form will be populated with your personal information. Verify that this information is correct, and click Continue.

5. Although establishing a seller's account is free, you will be asked to enter a credit-card number, the card's expiration date, and its identification number (the three-digit security code located on the back of your card), as shown in Figure 1.5. eBay uses this information to confirm that you are who you say you are—which helps protect buyers from dishonest types. The data will also be kept on file to pay for any eBay sellers' fees you accrue when you decide to post your first auction. Enter this information and click Continue.

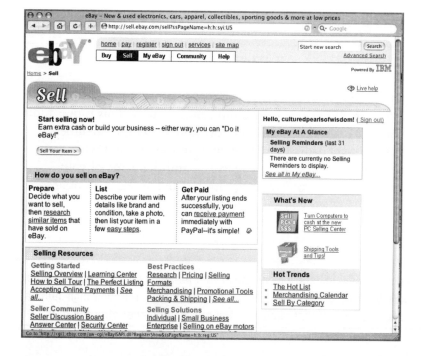

Figure 1.4

After you are logged in, you can click Sell and then Sell Your Item to quickly set up a seller's account.

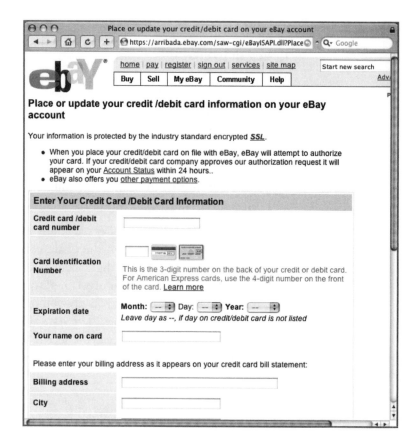

Figure 1.5

eBay doesn't charge you to sign up for a seller's account, but you must enter a credit-card number for identification.

6. eBay requires one final security step before you can become a seller: You must enter your checking-account information. This is one additional way eBay can verify your identify and keep other members safe; eBay does *not* deduct any money from this account when you sign up. Enter the name on your account and the name of your bank, and then enter your routing number and account number. Click Continue when you're finished.

Tip

If you don't know these numbers, look at one of your personal checks. On the bottom, where you see the row of numbers, the routing number is the nine-digit number before the dots, and the account number is the ten-digit number after the dots.

7. Now that you've entered two potential forms of payment, you have the option of selecting one of them as the default way to pay any fees you incur when you set up an auction. You must pay a nominal fee whenever you sell something on eBay, just like you would with any auction house or consignment shop. Click the radio button beside the form of payment you choose—either your credit card or your checking account. Then click Continue.

You're all set up to sell now. In fact, as soon as you complete your seller's account registration, you'll see links pointing you to the area where you can establish your first auction (Chapter 9 will walk you through this process). But don't go there just yet!

Preparing to Pay

Many buyers avoid exploring eBay's payment options until the last minute, when they're in the middle of paying for an auction they've won—which is when they realize that paying for an item on eBay may not be as straightforward as it is on other e-commerce sites. That's because many sellers on eBay are private or small-time entrepreneurs, and as such aren't equipped with merchant accounts to accept credit cards.

Fortunately, a number of Internet payment sites have popped up to let buyers and sellers safely and conveniently transmit money to one another. Buyers like using online payment services because

- They can pay for their auction purchase on the spot, by entering a credit card number or transferring cash directly from their bank account.

- They can keep their payment information private and secure.

- Sellers receive the buyer's payment quickly and don't need to wait for funds to clear before shipping the item.

Similarly, sellers tend to prefer online payment services because

- They can receive payments from buyers conveniently and quickly, without having to wait for the mail.

- Payments are guaranteed and usable right away, without needing to wait for checks to clear, so that they can ship products to buyers quickly.

- They can accept easy payments from buyers without the hassle and expense of a merchant credit card account.

PayPal

By far the most widely recognized and accepted online payment service is PayPal (http://www.paypal.com), shown in Figure 1.6. Now owned by eBay, PayPal has been on the scene long enough to be a nearly unanimous choice among sellers as the preferred form of auction payment. Sellers and buyers trust the PayPal site, and eBay makes using the service ultra-easy.

Figure 1.6

You can't go wrong with setting up a PayPal online payment account: It's the most widely accepted form of payment on eBay.

When you set up a PayPal account, you have the option of specifying whether you want to use a major credit card or funds from your checking account to pay for items you buy from eBay. Then, when it's time to pay a seller for the goodies you buy, you simply enter the seller's e-mail address and the amount you wish to pay. PayPal takes care of transferring the money into the seller's PayPal account. Because a third party is handling the transaction, sellers never see your personal or financial information. PayPal can also be used outside of eBay, to send payments to anybody who has an e-mail account.

Note

From time to time, you will run into a seller who doesn't accept PayPal. There are several other online payment services, including sites that allow you to send payment using wire transfers or money orders. See Chapter 7 for a list of these alternative services.

Establishing a PayPal Account

Before you get started buying and selling on eBay, take a moment to go ahead and set up a PayPal account just to have it handy. To register, do the following:

1. Visit http://www.paypal.com and click Send Money.

2. You will be asked to choose between a Personal or Professional account. For now, because you're just getting started, a personal account should suffice. Click the Personal Account option button and then select your country of residence from the pull-down menu. When you're finished, click Continue.

3. Enter your personal information, including your name, address, and phone number, as it is listed on your credit card or bank account. You'll also be asked to enter your e-mail address, a password, and answers to two security questions to help keep your account safe.

4. PayPal will send a verification e-mail message to your e-mail account. After you verify your account by clicking the link in the e-mail and enter your password, you're ready to enter your payment information to keep on file, as shown in Figure 1.7.

Figure 1.7

Your safest bet is to store a
credit card as your primary
source of payment for PayPal.

Caution

PayPal encourages you to enter a bank-account number from which it can withdraw money for your payment. Although the company assures you that this information is fully secure, PayPal *has* had some trouble in the past with hackers stealing bank-account and debit-card information from its customer databases. If this should ever happen again, you'll get your money back more quickly with a Visa, MasterCard, or other major credit card, which protects you from fraudulent activities, than if the cash comes directly out of your bank account.

Having said that, the only way PayPal allows you to become "verified" is for you to enter bank-account information. Being verified means that PayPal vouches for you—that your bank account confirms you are who you say you are. When dealing with high-ticket items, sellers might require this level of security before shipping to you, which means you may just have to grit your teeth and enter your bank-account information. Simply monitor your account withdrawals carefully if you plan to share this information.

5. For now, it's sufficient to enter a credit card as your form of payment. To do so, click My Account, and then click Add a Credit Card on the left navigation bar. Enter your account information, including the verification number (the three-digit number printed on the back of your credit card), and click Add Card. PayPal will immediately verify the card, a process that takes about 30 seconds.

Using Your PayPal Account as a Seller

If you plan to sell on eBay, you'll need a way for buyers to pay you for your items. Fortunately, the PayPal account you just set up enables you to both pay for purchases as well as collect money from your buyers. The only catch is that you'll need to upgrade your account to Premium status so you can accept payments. For now, your Personal account should suit you just fine. Later, as you become a more active seller, I'll walk you through the process of enhancing your account so you can make money rather than just spend it.

My eBay: Your Auction Headquarters

For everything you want to do on eBay, there's a handy place where you can manage it all: My eBay. This page, shown in Figure 1.8 and easily accessible at http://www.my.ebay.com, serves as your dashboard to help you view and manage your auctions, whether you're a buyer or seller. All your personal account information and payment information are also stored here. With My eBay, you can

- View items you're watching.
- See the current price and time left for items on which you're bidding.
- Watch bidding, see how much time is left in the auction, and see who the high bidders are for items you're selling.
- Save and manage your favorite searches.
- Manage your PayPal account.
- Change your shipping address and other personal information.

Figure 1.8

My eBay is your dashboard
for managing all your
eBay activities.

I'll spend more time talking about the abovementioned activities individually,
but for now know that My eBay is the page to which you can return if you
have just a few minutes to check on how all your auctions are performing.

chapter 2

Doing Your Homework

I know what you're thinking. Why do research? You know what you like when you see it. The details don't bother you as long as you have a piece that you love. Do the specifics really matter?

When it comes to jewelry, yes. Most of the materials that make up a piece of fine jewelry come from nature, so each piece is different. The variations and flaws of a piece can make the jewelry priceless—or worthless; so can the handiwork of a piece of jewelry, or the heritage of an antique piece. Even if you're buying or selling costume jewelry, if the piece is vintage, the designer, age, and quality of a piece mean so much. These are things that you can't always spot with an untrained eye, and they may well be the difference between a successful sale and one that's an unmitigated disaster.

As a buyer, rushing to a purchase without getting some background could cost you dearly if you end up with something that's less than you expected or, worse, something that ends up falling apart later. Educating yourself can also help you readjust your vision of what you want, which means you'll be happier in the long run.

Research is equally—if not more—important on the seller side, because sales of jewelry and watches are regulated by the Federal Trade Commission (FTC) and consumer protection laws. If you misrepresent a piece of jewelry or a watch that you're selling, you could open yourself up to fines, prosecution, or civil lawsuits. At the very least, you'll damage your reputation in the eBay community—and on eBay, reputation is everything.

What's the worst that could happen? Well, there have been a number of high-profile cases in the jewelry industry in the past ten years in which professional, expert, and well-meaning jewelry professionals have been sued, cited, or skewered on a news program by a roving undercover reporter because they misrepresented the jewelry they were selling. Although this is unlikely to happen to *you*, it's a good example of why you should do some legwork before you jump in to the tricky business of selling jewelry.

Research for Buyers

When you buy jewelry or watches online, you don't have the luxury of a jeweler or salesperson to explain things to you, so it's up to you to learn about what you're buying on your own. Bone up on some of the major guidelines before you even begin.

General Research

A few good resources, in print and on the Web, can give you a fast and basic education in jewelry shopping and buying, so you can get up to speed quickly.

Web Sites

The major jewelry industry associations sponsor educational Web sites that provide a down-and-dirty overview of shopping guidelines for the most popular kinds of jewelry. There's also an independent online guide thrown in for good measure.

■ **A Diamond Is Forever (http://www.adiamondisforever.com).** This site, shown in Figure 2.1, features an easy-to-understand overview of the 4Cs of diamonds, how they affect price, how to buy with a certificate, and why you need insurance. This is the official site of the New York City–based Diamond Information Center, which is the U.S. advertising arm of international diamond powerhouse De Beers.

■ **Jewelry Information Center (http://www.jic.org/buyingbasics).** Find basic tips on buying gold jewelry, watches, diamonds, cultured pearls, and platinum from the jewelry industry's premier public-relations organization.

Figure 2.1

This De Beers Web site allows you to design your own ring and explore the basics of shopping for and buying a diamond.

- **Cultured Pearl Information Center (http://www.pearlinfo.com/ consumer).** This thorough, illustrated guide to cultured-pearl varieties and quality characteristics is from this PR organization for the cultured pearl industry.

- **Add More Color to Your Life (http://www.addmorecolortoyourlife.com).** This site from the American Gem Trade Association features articles about different kinds of colored gemstones, including tips on buying them and news on fashion trends.

- **International Colored Gemstone Association (http://www.gemstone.org).** This site offers more background about colored gemstones and a beautiful image library featuring rare gems.

- **Platinum Guild International (http://www.preciousplatinum.com).** This buying guide, shown in Figure 2.2, features an explanation of setting types for rings, as well as recommendations for caring for the metal.

■ **Jewelry on About.com (http://jewelry.about.com).** A personal "guide" for this site manages a collection of links to articles about buying different kinds of gemstones and jewelry, including antiques, beads, costume jewelry, and gemstones.

Figure 2.2

The Platinum Guild International Web site, with the same clean, classy look as platinum itself, explains a thing or two about the precious metal.

Books

The following titles are essentials for establishing a library of reference books on jewelry.

■ **Gemstone Press titles.** This publishing company offers a series of helpful books written by jewelry expert Antoinette Matlins for consumers on how to buy various kinds of jewelry, including bridal jewelry, diamonds, colored gemstones, and cultured pearls. The books are practical and just specific enough to educate without confusing new jewelry consumers. A single book, *Jewelry & Gems: The Buying Guide*, offers illustrated examples of how to spot fakes and determine karat weight in gold jewelry. Figure 2.3 shows another of Matlins' books, *The Pearl Book*.

A Word About These Resources

The reference guides I recommend here won't steer you wrong, but they do all have one thing in common that seems at odds with your ultimate goal of buying or selling jewelry on eBay: Each one encourages you to shop at a jewelry store, specifically an independent jeweler, and *not* to shop on e-commerce sites or at online auctions. Why? Well, with so many different variables in the world of jewelry, it's hard for novice jewelry buyers to know what they're looking at when they shop. Because the associations that provide many of the resources I cite here represent the jewelry and gemstone industries, and because the authors of the books I note are charged with educating consumers, they want shoppers to have the best experience possible; sending them to a professional jeweler is their safest bet.

For occasions that really matter, when it's absolutely critical that you know exactly what you're getting, a professional retail jeweler is definitely a wise choice. This is someone who can guide you toward the style that will make you or your loved one happiest; who will help you care for, repair, and replace your jewelry through the ages; who will change your watch battery for free and look out for you as your tastes change.

That's not to say, however, that you should avoid online auctions and e-shopping altogether, despite what these resources say. You can become a savvy enough shopper to avoid the potholes on eBay *and* find a fantastic piece of jewelry for an exceptional price. And although you don't have that relationship to back you up, you'll no doubt be able to find a good, professional bench jeweler who can help with any upgrades, sizing, repairs, or maintenance you might need, and an expert appraiser should you want to insure or sell the jewelry later. So understand that when these references instruct you to avoid online auctions, they don't necessarily mean that *you*—an educated, cautious, and adventurous shopper—should avoid online auctions.

Tip

You may have noticed that I occasionally make reference to weights in terms of *carats* and *karats*. The difference can be confusing. Both terms are units of weight, but *carats* measure diamonds and gemstones, while *karats* refer to gold. So you'll have a 1-carat diamond (the equivalent of 0.2 grams), and 14-karat gold (which means 14 parts pure gold mixed with 10 parts alloy). So why are the terms so confusingly close? Well, both terms are actually derived from the Arabic word *carob*, which means *bean*—because beans were used as units of measurement for gems and metals centuries ago.

Figure 2.3

The Gemstone Press titles by Antoinette Matlins, including *The Pearl Book*, provide comprehensive education about different kinds of gemstones and jewelry.

- *Collectible Costume Jewelry: Identification and Values* by Cherri Simonds (Collector Books, 1997). If vintage costume jewelry is your thing, this book offers an overview of the various eras of fashion jewelry design, explanations of how to tell the difference between different kinds of styles, and how to read trademarks.

- **Fred Ward gem books.** If you're ga-ga for rubies or pearls or any other specific kind of gemstone, gem expert Fred Ward demystifies your passion. He has authored a number of books, each dedicated to the history, geological makeup, and buying ins and outs of a single type of gemstone.

Researching an Auction

So you've found it—that perfect Hamilton watch, the tourmaline ring your mother will love, or the pear-shaped diamond for which you've been searching high and low. It's right there on eBay, with crisp photos that make the piece shine and a lavish item description that confirms that this is the find you've been waiting for. The bidding is hot, and the price continues to climb by the hour.

At this point, you're dying to bid, but you know you should do some research first. How can you find out how this specific piece compares to what else is out there? Easy. Look no further than eBay itself. Here are some things you can do:

- **Look at other auctions in your category.** Browse the listings for other items that have approximately the same characteristics as the item you're looking at—similar size, color, age, or quality. How high are the bids going for those pieces?

- **Search completed auctions.** You can look for similar items that have already sold to get a historical perspective on how high these items tend to go. To do this, do the following:

  1. Click Search on the top navigation bar.

  2. Click More Search Options.

  3. In the page that appears (see Figure 2.4), type keywords related to the item you want (such as **Hamilton watch gold**) in the Enter keyword or item number field.

  4. Under that field, click the Completed Items Only check box to mark it.

  5. If desired, refine your search by limiting it to a range of prices, excluding certain keywords, or searching by seller's user ID.

  6. Click Search.

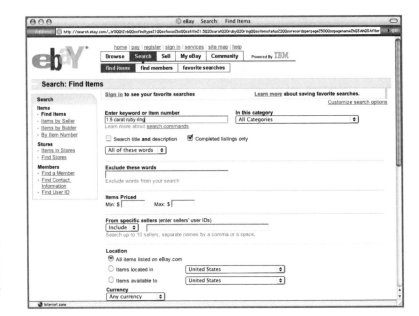

Figure 2.4

Search completed auctions to compare the item you're currently looking at to other items that have sold.

Note

eBay allows wildcard searches, which can help you find a range of sizes or descriptions without being precise in your keyword search. For example, if you're looking for other solitaire rings that contain diamonds close to 0.97 carats, type diamond ring 0.9* in the Enter keyword or item number field. The asterisk indicates you want a diamond that's in the 0.90 to 1 carat range.

■ **Study the seller's other items for sale.** Often, a jewelry seller will conduct many auctions simultaneously, all offering similar items. Take a look at how much the seller has out there, when the auctions are ending, and how high the prices are climbing. Often, you can find a practically identical item for a lower price if you're willing to wait a few more days.

■ **Visit or post to the eBay Community boards.** The eBay community is active, vocal, and surprisingly supportive. If you have a question about an item and need an objective and knowledgeable answer, the Discussion Boards are the place to go. You can post a question in the Jewelry section of the general Discussion Board, or you can join one of the 30 jewelry-related eBay's Collectors Clubs, where group members trade messages about specific topics or items.

If you still need more details, read on to learn about more resources available —more suited for sellers, but helpful for discriminating buyers too.

Research for Sellers

When you sell jewelry, especially if it's fine jewelry or vintage costume jewelry, your research needs to be more detailed, so you can best represent item quality and information to your potential buyers. Luckily, there are plenty of resources to help you more accurately price and describe your items for sale.

Online Communities

You'll be amazed at how helpful other jewelry buyers and sellers can be on the Internet. Tight-knit online communities can give you a glimpse into strategy and secrets, share helpful stories and tips, and provide support when you're struggling with a question. Here are a few places to start:

- **eBay Discussion Board and Sellers Groups (http://pages.ebay.com/ community).** Once again, the eBay community comes through. There's an extremely enthusiastic and supportive network of jewelry sellers, specializing in both fine and fashion jewelry, who don't mind helping newbies and veterans alike. This is a community interested in creating a fair marketplace and getting rid of deception—and ignorance —to level the playing field and build buyer trust. Post a digital photo of your item and your question about its authenticity, quality, and so on, on the Jewelry section of the general Discussion Board or Sellers Group, and watch how quickly you get feedback from your fellow sellers! Figure 2.5 shows the eBay Community page, where you can access various boards and groups.

- **DiamondTalk (http://www.diamondtalk.com).** This online community of diamond dealers, jewelers, and collectors is a useful resource for information about diamond jewelry and loose stones. You tend to find a lot of professionals here, which is good news for ensuring that the information you find here is accurate.

Figure 2.5

The eBay community is a helpful, supportive resource for researching items, whether you're a buyer or seller.

- **Ganoksin (http://www.ganoksin.com).** Ganoksin is one of the oldest jewelry communities online. It tends to be frequented by metalsmiths, bench jewelers, and jewelry designers—people who are into the intricacies of how jewelry is made. If you're looking to buy jewelry, you're not permitted to post questions about a specific piece; if, however, you're a seller, manufacturer, or designer, you can search the archives for unique information on jewelry-making and metalsmithing techniques.

- **TimeZone (http://www.timezone.com).** This online community, shown in Figure 2.6, includes discussions and reference materials for collectors, hobbyists, and watchmakers. The Public Forum and Auction Talk boards of the Watch Talk section will probably be the most helpful.

- **Delphi Forum (http://www.delphiforums.com).** This site is a collection of hundreds of forums set up by hobbyists and enthusiasts interested in any possible topic you could imagine. There are quite a few jewelry-related forums here, including discussions for collectors and traders of antique and estate jewelry, as well as jewelry-making boards. It's a great place to ask questions or seek opinions.

Figure 2.6

TimeZone is an online community for sellers and collectors to ask questions and share information about watches and timepieces.

Reference Web Sites

When it comes to research, the Internet is a beautiful thing. This is especially true with regard to researching jewelry authenticity and pricing. Here are a few places to start:

- **PriceScope (http://www.pricescope.com).** This diamond searching service, shown in Figure 2.7, advertises itself as an objective listing service. Here, you can enter a range of diamond characteristics (carat weight, color, clarity, and certification type) and receive a list of diamonds within that range from a number of different sources. This list includes the prices at which each piece is currently listed, which, as a seller, you can use to help determine your own prices. (Note that the prices in the list should not be used as hard-and-fast rule for pricing your goods, but as guidelines only; diamonds are not commodities and can sell within a range of prices.)

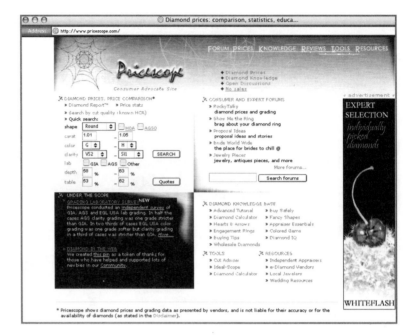

Figure 2.7

PriceScope provides an objective searchable database of diamond prices to help you determine what your diamond is worth.

- **Encyclopedia of Silver Marks (http://www.925-1000.com).** A labor of love by an antique silver dealer, this online reference guide contains more than 2,500 marks from the U.S., Great Britain, and France, as well as from major design houses such as Tiffany and Georg Jensen.

- **Researching Costume Jewelry (http://www.illusionjewels.com/costumejewelrymarks.html).** This site features an illustrated guide to some of the most popular manufacturers of vintage costume jewelry, characteristics of the jewelry they made, and what their marks looked like, to help you accurately identify the piece you're selling.

Books

Sellers will find the following titles essential:

- *The Official Identification and Price Guide to Antique Jewelry* by **Arthur Guy Kaplan (House of Collectibles, 1990).** With a reputation as the most comprehensive guide to antique and estate jewelry in the industry, this guide, shown in Figure 2.8, includes photographs and explanations covering jewelry periods and types from 1750 to 1950.

Figure 2.8

Arthur Guy Kaplan's antique jewelry identification and price guide covers jewelry periods spanning two hundred years.

- *Warman's Jewelry* by Christie Romero (Krause Publications, 2002). The Warman's books, which are designed to educate and serve as reference materials on all kinds of antiques, are well known. This book, now in its third edition, covers 18th-, 19th-, and 20th-century fine and costume jewelry with colorful illustrations.

- *Gem Identification Made Easy* by Antoinette L. Matlins and Antonio C. Bonanno (Gemstone Press, 2003). Another title from Gemstone Press, this book serves hard-core sellers and hobbyists. You don't necessarily need to be a professional to use it, but it will provide helpful guidelines for spotting synthetics, understanding gemstone treatments, and knowing when to contact a real appraiser.

■ *Simon & Schuster's Guide to Gems and Precious Stones* by C. Ciprianai and A. Borelli (Fireside Books, 1986). This title is popular among gem hobbyists and dealers, and provides explanations and illustrations to help you understand gemstone characteristics.

Putting Your Research to Use

Ever heard the old adage that a little education can be a dangerous thing? If you're just getting started, these books and guides will give you enough information to enlighten you, but that doesn't mean you're an expert. You still need to proceed with caution, remembering that when it comes to the world of jewelry—fine or costume—there will always be something that can surprise you. The rest of this book will help you read between the lines as a buyer, represent yourself accurately as a seller, and reap the full benefits of the wide, wild, wonderful world of eBay jewelry and watches.

part 2

chapter 3

The eBay World Is Your
Oyster (or Diamond Mine)

Now that you're armed and dangerous with an eBay user ID, a payment account, and a little knowledge about what you're looking for, it's time to set out to explore eBay's jewelry categories. Before you start, however, a gentle warning: Beware the emotional pull of the things you'll see. Viewing jewelry on eBay is not at all like seeing it in a jewelry store. True, it's not as beautiful when it isn't sparkling under bright white lights. But on eBay, it's all laid out before you, easily accessible, with the prices, or the potential prices, prominently displayed and no intimidating glass case between you and the goods. Somehow, it seems more attainable. And depending on how soon the auction is ending, and how sleep-deprived you are when you're looking at it, the auction you've stumbled upon might clearly seem to be your *perfect* jewelry purchase…

…Until it arrives. Remember that, unlike with retail stores, there may not be as much room for buyer's remorse with eBay. Once again, the path to avoiding buying blues involves research, a thorough understanding of the eBay auction rules and processes, and finally, some careful attention paid to your worrisome inner voice.

Okay, enough of the cautions. Let's go have some fun.

The Many Faces of Jewelry on eBay

For many people, especially Americans, the first thing that pops to mind when they think of jewelry is *finished jewelry*, especially the kind with diamonds: earrings, bracelets, and of course, the diamond engagement ring. Beyond that, most jewelry stores stock some basic gold lockets and chains; a standard offering of emerald, sapphire, and ruby rings and pendants; your basic birthstone selection; and a few strands of white cultured pearls. But in the United States, when it comes to jewelry, diamonds reign supreme.

Things are different on eBay. Oh, you'll see diamonds—lots of them. From one-of-a-kind loose stones of many carats in weight, to bargain-priced channel-set rings or solitaire necklaces, there is no shortage of diamonds on eBay. Many eBay sellers are professional diamond dealers, including those with offices in diamond districts in New York, Los Angeles, and other major cities. So if you're in the market for a breathtaking rock, this might be the place to find it. (See Figure 3.1.)

Figure 3.1

Diamond engagement rings are among the most popular buys on eBay. Photo by Robert Weldon, courtesy of Gemological Institute of America.

But there's much more to eBay jewelry than that. In fact, eBay is an exotic and unparalleled bazaar of everything gemological, geological, and metal-lurgical. In layman's terms, there are treasures here to stretch the limits of your imagination. Here is a glimpse at some of the things you might find:

- Gemstones in every color of the spectrum, mined from every corner of the earth

- Luscious pearls cultured in the steamy waters of the South Sea

- Art Deco filigreed brooches

- 22-karat gold rings painstakingly embellished with Greek-style granulation

- Complex wristwatches engineered so precisely that they keep time to the microsecond

But of course, such abundance can yield confusion. If you're not yet a jewelry connoisseur, deciphering the many different categories and subcategories—more than 250 in all—can be harrowing. Let me briefly introduce you to what you'll find when you began to explore the Jewelry & Watches categories on eBay.

Finding Jewelry by Category on eBay

Browsing can be fun, but also frustrating if you don't know exactly how to find what you're looking for. Here's a brief guide on how to navigate the thousands of jewelry-related listings on eBay:

1. From http://www.ebay.com, click the Buy tab to see eBay's complete list of main categories. If no Buy tab is present, look for a list of categories on the left side of the page.

2. In the list of categories, click Jewelry & Watches. When you do, you'll see a long—and somewhat overwhelming—list of subcategories.

3. Click these subcategory links to drill down one, two, or even three more levels. As you click into the sublevels, you are narrowing your selection, becoming more specific about what you're browsing.

In general, the main headers in the eBay Jewelry & Watches section refer to a *type* of jewelry, such as bracelets, necklaces, or rings. Mixed in with those broad headings are broad style categories, such as Men's Jewelry or Tribal Jewelry. Other headers refer more to how the jewelry is sold—as a set or part of a lot as opposed to as an individual piece. Although there's seemingly no rhyme or reason to this way of categorizing, it does best reflect how consumers traditionally have shopped for jewelry.

A sample path as you drill down into categories might take you through Bracelets > Diamond > Tennis Bracelets. In this example, you're drilling down from type of jewelry, into the materials that make it up, and then into style.

Category Primer

How can you find what you're looking for as quickly as possible? Here's a primer of what each eBay Jewelry category contains:

- **Bracelets.** Bracelets in this category are all fine jewelry of some kind, whether cubic zirconia set in gold, silver with semi-precious gemstones such as peridot, or much more luxurious pieces. This is the category where you can look for your understated diamond tennis bracelet, a shiny silver toggle bracelet, or even that platinum and emerald cuff you're dying to wear on New Year's Eve.

- **Charms & Charm Bracelets.** Subcategories in this category enable you to drill down into Italian modular charm bracelets—which are made up of links, or plates, that slide into one another—and the traditional charm bracelets you remember from your youth, with charms that hook onto a ringed bracelet. The bracelets and individual charms are grouped together in each subcategory. Clicking Other gives you more of the same from both the Italian and Traditional categories.

- **Designer, Artisan Jewelry.** This category is a bit of a hodgepodge. In the Beaded, Lampwork section, you'll find jewelry made by designers who specialize in using glass and gemstone beads. These are typically *not* fine jewelry, though you might find beads made out of semi-precious stones such as amethyst. In other subcategories, though, you'll stumble upon fine jewelry marked with names you'll recognize —Tiffany & Co., Cartier, Lagos, David Yurman, and other trendy designers such as Me & Ro. This is the category you'll need to approach with some skepticism, as there have been many documented cases of fakes sold here. Chapter 4, "The Ins and Outs of Jewelry Buying," will give you a better idea of how to tell the real from the bogus.

■ **Earrings.** As with the Bracelets category, you'll find mostly fine jewelry mixed with a few price-point options here. Earrings come in every possible variation—gold, silver, or platinum only; precious and semi-precious gemstones; diamonds; and synthetic stones such as cubic zirconia and moissanite. In this category, you'll locate your diamond studs, exquisite briolette "chandelier" earrings, dainty gold hoops, and any other variation.

■ **Ethnic, Tribal Jewelry.** This is another category that's all over the place, with a mix of Tibetan beads, Celtic symbols, Native American turquoise, African wooden beads and carvings, and Mexican silver. As shown in Figure 3.2, it's a fun category to browse, because you're never quite sure what you'll find.

Figure 3.2

In the Ethnic jewelry category, you'll find items as diverse as African headdresses, jadeite beads, and other styles with a strong heritage behind them.

■ **Fashion Jewelry.** By its very definition, fashion jewelry can be anything. Its stones and metals don't have to be "real" or natural. So here you'll find affordable, pretty jewelry that doesn't necessarily adhere to any standards—the metal can be "silvertone" instead of silver, and the sparkly adornments are typically crystals. However, thrown into the mix, you'll generally find some more precious offerings. It's a free-for-all, but if you're simply looking for a fun pair of earrings or brooch to wear and don't necessarily care about value or authenticity, this is definitely a good category to browse.

■ **Jewelry Boxes & Supplies.** Here you'll find jewelry cleaners, jewelry boxes, jewelers' tools, and findings (which include clasps, wire, and other things that bench jewelers, or people who make and repair jewelry, use). People who are venturing into making their own jewelry frequent this category to find good deals on the many items they need. If you're thinking about becoming a seller, this is also a good place to look for diamond testers, jewelers' loupes, and other tools you might need.

■ **Loose Beads.** Another category popular among crafty types, this is a place to find individual or groups of ceramic, glass, gemstone, and wooden beads for your designs.

■ **Loose Gemstones.** This is an important category for jewelry buyers because it represents a huge part of what has made eBay, and Internet jewelry sales, so popular in the first place. Often, buyers who want the perfect ring work with a jeweler to design a unique setting. The fact is, however, that it's often less expensive to buy the center gemstone someplace else rather than working directly with the retail store and paying the markup. That's why you find so many loose gemstones, including diamonds, on eBay. Likewise, if you simply collect loose stones, you'll find plenty of beautifully cut, unusual, and fascinating stones here, like the cut golden beryl shown in Figure 3.3. One thing to keep an eye out for here are the "lots" of gemstones, as well as those advertised as "rough" or "unpolished." I'll talk more about those in Chapter 4.

Figure 3.3

Unique gemstones such as this beautifully cut piece of golden beryl are available in the eBay Loose Gemstones category. Photo by Mike Havstad, courtesy of Gemological Institute of America.

- **Men's.** It might seem funny that men's jewelry merits such an itsy bitsy category, but truthfully, men's jewelry has traditionally been a low-profile one in the jewelry industry. When you look at the numbers, though, this might seem unjustified—a recent study by MVI Marketing showed 75 percent of men surveyed wore non-bridal jewelry. If you're shopping for yourself or for a gift, this might be an eBay category to check out—you can find chains, bracelets, rings, cufflinks, tie clasps, and more.

- **Necklaces.** From gold chains and diamond pendants to exotic baubles of amber, jade, or onyx, the Necklaces category features thousands of necklace styles.

- **Rings.** When you look at the list of categories, Rings appears to be the smallest, with only three subcategories listed underneath. Don't be fooled, however! Diamond rings are one of the most shopped-for items on eBay. Like the jewelry listed in the Necklaces, Earrings, and Bracelets categories, much of the jewelry offered for auction in Rings is brand new; it's typically for sale because it's old or closeout inventory, or because its dealer otherwise needs to move it quickly.

- **Sets.** If you like to be coordinated, this is the category for you. Here, you'll find matching necklace and earring sets and coordinated bridal ring sets. Fine and fashion jewelry tend to be sold alongside each other in this category.

- **Vintage, Antique.** Generally speaking, the jewelry in this category was made prior to the 1980s. There's a huge market for vintage and antique jewelry in the fine and costume categories, and most of these coveted pieces will be found here. *Antique* jewelry refers to jewelry made more than one hundred years ago, such as the piece shown in Figure 3.4, while *vintage* jewelry refers to jewelry that's pre-owned but was made between the 1910s and the 1970s. This is where you'll find everything from Edwardian to Art Deco to post–World War II styles.

- **Watches.** At first glance, this appears to be a small category, but drill down to find a whole world of pocket watches, wristwatches, accessories, and watchmaking tools. According to eBay, 70 percent of the watches for sale here are brand new, representing the best-known watch brands: Rolex, Cartier, Patek Philippe, Omega, and Tag Heuer. But this is also a place where you can find priceless collectibles— one-of-a-kind watches that sell for tens and hundreds of thousands of dollars to hungry collectors.

Figure 3.4

Antique and vintage jewelry from throughout the ages is available at eBay. Photo by Harold and Erica van Pelt, courtesy of Gemological Institute of America.

- **Wholesale Lots.** When liquidation companies purchase assets, they can end up with large quantities of jewelry, which the merchants in this category choose to sell as one large grouping of items. Wholesale lots can be interesting because you never quite know what you'll get. Often, lots consist of several dozen sterling silver rings or body jewelry, all of different styles; picking over the lot when it arrives can be half the fun of winning.

Caution

Beware lots that promise "treasure chests" with hundreds of carats of gemstones—unless you're simply looking for a colorful grab bag for kids. Sometimes dealers or collectors purchase huge lots of rough stones and then pick out the very best gems for themselves. eBay is a good way to offload what's left—which are usually "commercial grade," or low-quality, gemstones. It's fairly safe to assume that if prices are very low for a "treasure chest" lot, the true treasures have probably already been removed by somebody who knows what to look for.

Smart Browsing

Browsing is like window-shopping. You idly sift through what's posted on the site to see what's there, what's priced reasonably, and what might pique your interest. As opposed to searching (which I'll talk about in a moment), browsing is typically an activity for buyers who have money to spend but don't necessarily know what they want. It's also a fun way to while away the few spare minutes between meetings at work or before you go to bed at night.

Of course, once you become familiar with the categories, you might find yourself returning to a handful of them again and again—clicking four or five times to find these categories, and then cruising through all the listings you've already seen to find what's new. Here are a few suggestions to help you refine your technique for more efficient and successful browsing:

- **Bookmark categories.** If you find yourself fascinated by the unique items in the Vintage, Antiques category, or if rings are your thing, simply add that category's main page to your Favorites or Bookmarks in your Web browser. Most browsers even allow you to position your favorite links on your toolbar so you can get to the page in one quick click. (For instructions on bookmarking a page, see your Web browser's Help information.) Alternatively, add the category to your My Favorite Categories list by clicking Add to My Favorite Categories at the top of the category page; you can access your My Favorite Categories list from your My eBay page.

■ **Sort by new listings.** As Figure 3.5 shows, auction listings are divided into columns, with each column listing a vital piece of information about the auction. You can click these column headers to sort the listings so you see them in a particular order. For example, you might click the Time Listed header to sort the listings so you see the most recently listed items first (the heading title will toggle to Time Left after you click it). This is useful if you are familiar with the subcategory and wish to bypass the auctions that have been posted for several days and just see the newest additions to the category. Alternatively, click the down arrow next to the Sort by field above the headers and choose Time: newly listed from the menu that appears.

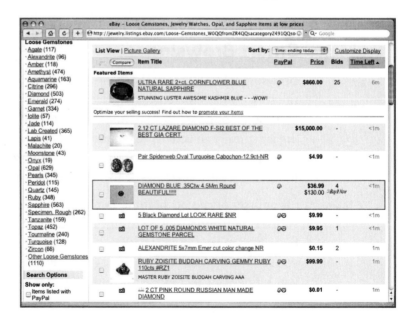

Figure 3.5

The headers in the columns of auction listings are clickable, allowing you to sort by criteria in that column.

■ **Sort by end time.** On the other hand, if you haven't visited a category in awhile and you're curious about what you might be able to snatch up for a steal, you might be interested in seeing the auctions that are ending in the next few minutes. In the far right column, click the Time Listed header so it reads Time Left (or choose Time: ending soonest from the Sort by menu). Suddenly, all the auctions that are ending in the next few minutes or hours will jump to the top of your list, giving you a shot at a last-minute winning bid.

Seek and You Shall Find

The major advantage of shopping on eBay is selection. But that same advantage can also become overwhelming when you set out to find a piece that suits your taste and budget. You can browse the categories I mentioned above all day, and you still might not find precisely what you're looking for—especially if you have a clear idea of what you want. Here are some tips for unearthing what you really want.

Search Simplicity

When you just want to see what's out there, the easiest, fastest way to find what you're looking for is to search. As shown in Figure 3.6, there are two places from which you can search eBay:

■ A search field is located at the top right of every page on eBay, so no matter how far you've drilled down into a category, you can type in keywords and search the whole site.

■ As you browse different categories and subcategories, a search field is located at the top of the list of items in the category you're browsing. This search field defaults to searching within the designated category, although you can use the pull-down menu to jump to another level and search a broader base of items.

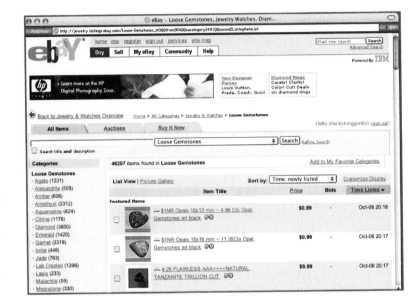

Figure 3.6

You can quickly access
search from one of two places:
in the upper right-hand
corner of the screen, or at
the top of the auction
listing within a category.

Focusing Your Search

When you type keywords into either of these search fields, eBay returns a
list of items whose descriptions contain the word or words you enter. The
fewer keywords you use, the more results you'll pull up. If you find you're
pulling up too many results to digest them easily, you can focus your search
using a few simple techniques:

■ **Using wildcards.** As noted in Chapter 2, "Doing Your Homework,"
eBay enables you to perform wildcard searches, which can help you
find a range of sizes or descriptions. For example, if you're looking
for other solitaire rings that contain diamonds close to 0.97 carats,
type **diamond ring 0.9*** in the search field. The asterisk indicates
you want a diamond that's in the 0.90 to 1 carat range.

■ **Using quotation marks.** If you're searching for an item listing
containing an exact phrase, type the phrase in the search field, and
surround the phrase with quotation marks. This is useful particularly
when you want a product that has an exact brand name or proper
style name associated with it. For example, a search for **"Hampden
Molly Stark pocket watch"** will help you look for only the Hampden
brand, the Molly Stark design, and the pocket watch style of this
antique timepiece.

If you're still having trouble narrowing your results, try conducting an Advanced Search. Advanced Searches can help you if you're looking for very specific items or information. To conduct an Advanced Search, either click Advanced Search in the top-right area of any eBay page, or click Refine Search next to the search field at the top of a category auction listing and then click More Search Options. Doing so opens the Advanced Search screen, shown in Figure 3.7.

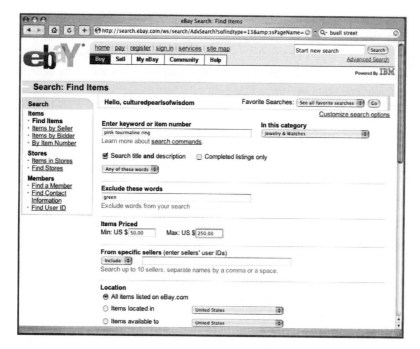

Figure 3.7

Advanced Search allows you to narrow your search by pulling results from established price ranges, geographic locations, and other criteria.

Here's a guide to using eBay's Advanced Search feature:

1. In the Enter keyword or item number field, enter a keyword or a series of keywords, or enter an item number if you know it.

Tip

eBay assigns a ten-digit number to each individual auction. This is the eBay item number. You'll need to know this item number if you are juggling multiple bids or sales, or if you ever need to contact a buyer or seller about a particular auction.

2. From the In this category pull-down menu, select the category and, if available, the subcategory to which you want to limit your search.

3. Click the Search title and description check box to select it if you want eBay's search engine to look for keywords in the listing title as well as in the content of the listing description. If you want to search the title only, leave the box unchecked.

Tip

When you first search for items, it's probably best to check the Search title and description check box so you can make your search as broad as possible. Only if you're looking for a very specific type of item, or are simply getting too many search results, should you limit your search to title only.

4. If you're looking for items that have already sold (for example, if you're researching price history for similar items), click the Completed items only check box to select it.

5. To further narrow your search, select whether you want to search for any of the words (for more results), all of the words (for fewer results), or the exact phrase (for even fewer results).

6. Enter any words you want to exclude from your search. For example, if you want to search for tourmaline jewelry, but you're more interested in green tourmaline than in pink tourmaline, type **pink** in the Exclude these words field.

7. To enter your price range, type a number in both the Min and Max fields in the Items Priced section.

8. If you want to search only for items by a particular seller, type his or her seller ID in the From specific sellers field and make sure Include is selected in the corresponding pull-down menu. Alternatively, if you want to omit items from the seller from your search results, choose Exclude from the pull-down menu.

9. To limit the search to items located in a particular country, select the Items located in option button and choose the country from the corresponding pull-down menu.

10. To limit the search to items available in a particular country, select the Items available to option button and choose the country from the corresponding pull-down menu.

11. To limit the search to sellers who accept only a particular currency, select that currency from the Currency pull-down menu.

12. Narrow your search to include only those auctions where sellers are auctioning multiple, identical items by entering a minimum, exact, or maximum number of items.

13. If you're interesting in picking up an item or receiving a shipped item quickly, you can search for items being auctioned by sellers within a certain distance from your home. Enter your ZIP or postal code, and then select a distance from the pull-down menu to search within a certain mile radius from your location.

14. Check the next three boxes if you wish to search only auctions that offer a Buy It Now option, only auctions whose sellers accept PayPal, or only auctions that are gift items (which often means that sellers will gift-wrap the item, offer express shipping, or ship directly to a gift recipient).

15. Finally, select how you want to sort your search results—by time, price, or distance—and the number of results you want displayed per page.

16. Click Search to see your results.

Tip

If your search returns too few items, you can return to the Advanced Search page and enter fewer criteria to broaden the search.

Saving Your Favorite Searches

If you're constantly on the lookout for a certain kind of piece, you can save your Advanced Search criteria and even instruct eBay to e-mail you when an item matching your criteria is posted. Here's how:

1. On the search results page that appears after you conduct your Advanced Search, click Add to Favorites in the top-right corner of the page (see Figure 3.8).

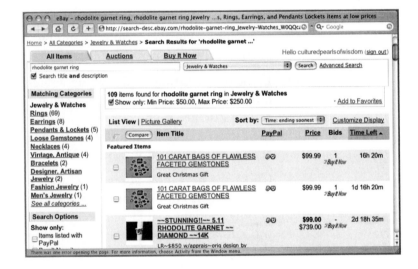

Figure 3.8

Saving a search is easy. After you get your search results, simply click Add to Favorites at the top right of the results page.

2. Double-check to make sure your search criteria are correct.

3. If you want to be notified each day about newly listed items that fall within your search criteria, click the Email me daily check box to select it.

4. Select the period of time for which you wish to receive these e-mail notifications.

5. Click Save Search. Your favorite searches are accessible from your My eBay page, as shown in Figure 3.9.

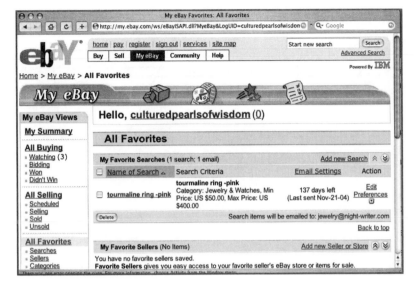

Figure 3.9

Manage your favorite searches using the dashboard on My eBay.

How to Decipher an Auction

Whether you prefer to search for auctions or to browse categories, when you find an auction that looks interesting, you simply click the auction's link to view it. No matter what type of item an auction features, the auction's page will contain the following information (see Figure 3.10):

- Product description
- Current price of the item
- Amount of time left in the auction
- Number of bids so far
- Shipping and handling charges
- Seller name and number of feedback replies
- PowerSeller icon
- Feedback percentage
- Link to eBay store

Seller name and number of feedback replies

PowerSeller icon

Product description

Current price of the item

Amount of time left

Number of bids so far

Shipping and handling charges

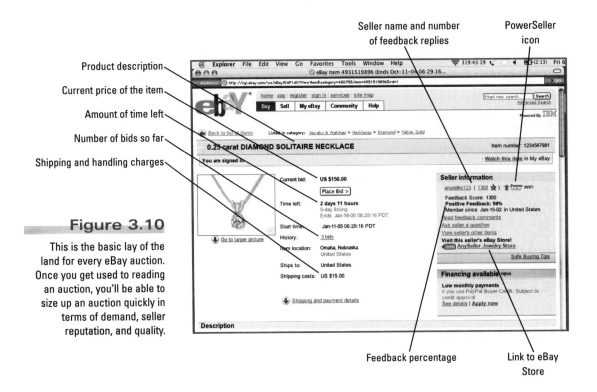

Figure 3.10

This is the basic lay of the land for every eBay auction. Once you get used to reading an auction, you'll be able to size up an auction quickly in terms of demand, seller reputation, and quality.

Feedback percentage

Link to eBay Store

Chapter 4 will help you decide whether the item listed is right for you. Read on!

chapter 4

The Ins and Outs of Jewelry Buying

This is where your job as an eBay buyer gets tricky. You're beginning to get a feel for the landscape, but when you start to dig a little deeper, you become overwhelmed by the huge discrepancies in what you're seeing. One-carat diamonds priced at 25%, and others selling for $9,000. Strands of cultured pearls or ruby bracelets, marked with retail prices of thousands of dollars, with high bids of three and four dollars apiece. Priceless names such as Tiffany, Cartier, and Bulgari, all selling for rock-bottom prices, while a simple pair of gold earrings is fetching more than a hundred dollars at auction. What's going on here? How can these sellers part with jewelry that you'd see in the stores tagged with mind-boggling prices for a few measly bucks? Is it all too good to be true?

A Few Simple Rules of Bargain-Hunting

The answer is: yes and no. It's true that there's almost always a reason that a piece of jewelry is priced so low. As with any other channel, sellers use eBay to turn a profit. That seller isn't listing a South Sea cultured pearl necklace that could fetch $12,000 in a jewelry store for $2.50 out of the kindness of her heart. You've got to be sure that sellers are making money somehow, or at least trying to recover their investments, even if prices are unbelievably low. Typically, when you see one of these deals, one of the following factors is at work:

■ **The seller bought the jewelry cheap himself.** Often, sellers will luck into opportunities such as massive closeouts, liquidations, or estate sales. So even if the jewelry is inherently valuable, the seller might have purchased it for pennies on the dollar, and can afford to price it low.

■ **An international seller has access to locally produced jewelry.** In some overseas markets, jewelry is in abundance. Take certain parts of Asia, for example. Historically, cultured freshwater pearls, like the ones shown in Figure 4.1, have been overproduced and are therefore abundant in China. The best of these pearls are often snatched up by international dealers looking for a good deal; then local dealers seek a way to offload the lesser-quality goods. The same is true for colored gemstones that are cut and polished—as well as jewelry that is manufactured—locally in China and Thailand. Jewelry might be priced lower because import/export fees have not yet been tacked on, and because of the exchange rate. Access to these pearls might save you a lot of money, but be careful that you're not buying the overproduced, lower-quality dreck that some of these sellers might be trying to move.

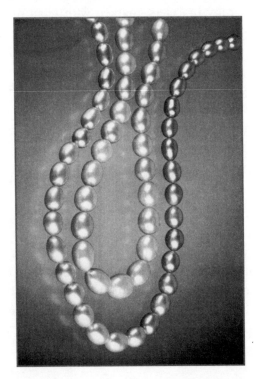

Figure 4.1

In certain countries, sellers can offload gemstones and jewelry, like these freshwater pearls, for staggeringly low prices. Photo by Maha Tannous, courtesy of the Gemological Institute of America.

- **The jewelry isn't as valuable as it first appears.** It could be because the stones are synthetic or of poor quality, or because the piece is poorly made. The seller might reveal this clearly in the description—or not. You'll need to learn to read between the lines and understand some common terminology.

- **The jewelry is counterfeit or a reproduction.** Again, the seller may choose to reveal this in the description, or not. Keep your eyes open for signs.

On the other hand, you may also see pieces for sale that have a higher starting price or reserve—the set price below which the seller won't sell the item—than others. Whether you see a pair of earrings selling for a few hundred dollars, or a diamond ring selling for several thousand, there are some things you might assume about these pieces:

- **You're very possibly getting a deal.** Even though the price tag seems high, like the one shown in Figure 4.2, it's likely that the listed price is still lower than you'd pay in a retail store. The seller may be a professional, either a wholesaler seeking other channels to offload goods or a retail jeweler who wants to move dusty old inventory. Either way, you're probably going to save serious money, even if the price initially gives you sticker shock.

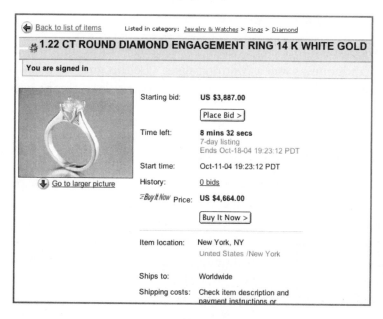

Figure 4.2

The price for this ring might be unbelievably high, but believe it or not, it's probably priced lower than it would be offline.

■ **The piece is possibly more accurately represented.** In other words, you can probably feel a little safer that the piece is what the seller says it is—that it's a real diamond, the designer hallmark is real, and the quality is high.

■ **Your seller will probably be more flexible with you.** Chances are, you're more likely to have leeway in terms of returns if the piece doesn't suit your fancy or isn't what you expected. Although it's not always the case, the sellers who list higher-priced auctions are often professionals who have a real business behind them, and who are more versed in establishing fair terms with their customers. You're also probably going to have more protection shopping in this range, with insurance and fraud-protection programs backing you up.

These points are sweeping generalizations, and are only meant as guidelines. As a buyer, you need to learn how to shop for jewelry and what to expect—indeed, demand—before you decide to bid. It will ultimately be up to you to decide whether you're getting a great deal. But if you go into eBay buying with one mantra in mind, it's this one: If it seems too good to be true, it quite possibly is—maybe. As nebulous as that might seem, it's part of the fun of eBay. Finding an honest deal is part of the hunt.

Shopping Guide

This section provides you with a few guidelines for selecting jewelry—must-haves from a quality standpoint as well as warning signs. Use this guide as a basic introduction. For more detailed information on any particular category, you might want to do your own research.

Diamonds and Diamond Jewelry

Despite their reputation for mystery and romance, diamonds are perhaps the easiest type of jewelry to shop for due to the sheer amount of information that has been dealt to diamond consumers. Still, with the diamond industry constantly changing and the introduction of new technologies to treat real diamonds and create simulants, you should prepare yourself for what you'll see on eBay.

Assessing Quality

Anybody who has ever shopped for diamonds has learned what the industry calls the 4Cs: carat, clarity, color, and cut. These four pillars of quality are the best way to understand and shop for diamonds. Here's what to look for:

- **Carat.** Many people think that *carat* refers to the size of the diamond, but it's actually a measurement of weight. One carat is the equivalent of 0.2 grams, or a little more than 0.007 ounces. Diamonds less than one carat in weight are usually measured in points—for example, a 70-point diamond is the same as a 0.70-carat diamond. Keep in mind that price typically jumps disproportionately once you hit one carat and above, so price-minded buyers often look for diamonds that fall just below one carat in size. Also understand that bigger isn't always better. It's preferable to have a smaller but better-cut diamond than a bigger, poorly cut one.

- **Clarity.** This is a measure of the flaws, or *inclusions*, in a diamond. Diamonds that come out of the ground aren't always clear and perfect; sometimes you'll find fissures and cracks or streaks of black carbon in the middle of the stone. Cutters do their best to cut and polish the diamond so the inclusions don't show to the naked eye, but sometimes it can't be helped. The more visible the inclusion is without a loupe (a jeweler's magnifying glass), the less valuable the diamond is. Clarity grades are indicated by the codes VVS (very, very slight), VS (very slight), SI (slightly included), and I (included), with varying steps between each one.

- **Color.** Color grades are measured using letters of the alphabet, although strangely, the grading scale starts with the letter D, signifying colorless, and descends from there. You can generally think of grades in groups of three. For example, there's little discernable difference between a D and an F diamond; similarly, you'll get about the same color with a G as you will with an I. The lower the color grade, the more of a yellow color you'll start to see, but the yellow doesn't really start to appear noticeably until you get into J colors and below. A diamond that rates D or E will cost a pretty penny.

■ **Cut.** This fourth C is often misunderstood. People either think it means the *shape* of a diamond— pear shape, round, marquis, and so forth—or the type or style of cut, such as the brilliant cut, a method of cutting that creates 58 different facets on a diamond. In fact, *cut* refers to the care with which the diamond cutter shaped the various facets, angles, and dimensions of a diamond so the maximum amount of light can shine through it, thus creating that spectacular, colorful sparkle for which diamonds are known. A diamond with a cut that's too deep or too shallow loses light and brilliance, and is not as valuable as a well-cut diamond.

Many experts will tell you that cut is the single most important characteristic on which to judge a diamond. Unfortunately, cut is the one characteristic that's hardest to determine without seeing the diamond first-hand, since there's no real grading scale to help you judge cut. Scientific types love to figure out the quality of the cut by studying dimensions of various parts of the diamond—identified in Figure 4.3 —but unless you really know what you're talking about, it's hard to use all these measurements and percentages to determine whether your diamond will be beautiful.

Figure 4.3

Although there's no standard for grading diamond cut, those who care deeply about the fourth C study the dimensions of the diamond. These include the depth of a diamond, the diameter of its table (the top, flat part), the angles of the facets on its crown (the more substantial top half of the diamond), the thickness of its girdle (the band that encircles the widest part of the diamond), and the depth of its pavilion (the lower, "pointy" part).

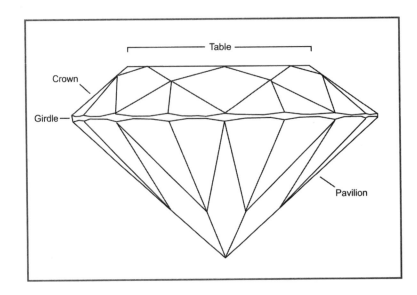

Note

One term with which you should familiarize yourself is *ideal cut,* which is the term used for a diamond with perfect dimensions. Ideal cut diamonds will often cost about 15 or 20 percent more than comparable diamonds that are not ideal cut. You'll want to make sure the seller produces a certificate (see the next section) proving the diamond is ideal cut before you invest your time and money in buying it.

When all is said and done, a diamond grade will look something like this:

1.2 carat E VS1

Translation: The diamond is 1.2 carats in weight, E in color (which means the stone is almost colorless), and is very slightly included, meaning you won't be able to see the inclusions with your eyes. Depending on how it's cut, this would be a desirable diamond.

Buying with a Certificate

If the diamond jewelry you're buying contains larger stones or a prominent center or single stone, your seller should sell the piece accompanied by a certificate from a gemological laboratory, such as the one shown in Figure 4.4. Diamond dealers send their diamonds to these independent gem labs, which examine them and provide objective, official evaluations of the diamonds' quality. They document the diamonds' grades on paper certificates, which dealers then use to "certify" each diamond's quality when selling it to a customer.

You won't find certificates for diamond jewelry that uses many smaller stones, such as with a tennis bracelet, pavé ring, or diamond-studded brooch. But if you're purchasing diamond stud earrings, a diamond solitaire pendant, or especially a diamond ring, you'll want to look for sellers that ship certificates with their wares. Often, eBay sellers will include a scanned image of certificates in their auction descriptions. When bidding, be sure to download a copy of the image of the certificate and match it up with the certificate that comes with the jewelry when you receive it.

Figure 4.4

Laboratory certificates, such
as this certificate from
the gemological lab GIA,
should accompany any
piece of diamond jewelry
with a major central stone.

Certificates typically come from one of a handful of recognized gemological labs around the world. These include the Gemological Institute of America (GIA), European Gemological Laboratories (EGL), American Gem Society (AGS), and International Gemological Institute (IGI). Although there are other independent gem labs that might certify diamonds, these are the most common acronyms you'll see.

Note

There are countless stories about dishonest sellers who mismatch certificates with stones. In other words, they send a real certificate made for a *good* diamond to accompany a *bad* one and hope the buyer won't be any the wiser. If you believe your diamond doesn't match the certificate you receive, take it to an independent appraiser to make sure. If the stone and the certificate indeed don't match up, ask your seller for a refund, and report him to eBay if necessary. See Chapter 8, "The Good, the Bad, and the Ugly," for more details.

Red Flags

You'll see it all on eBay, from rock-bottom prices to staggeringly high ones, with sexy descriptions and photos designed to entice even the wariest buyer. This is all the more reason to never forget the "too good to be true" philosophy, and to keep your eyes open for red flags indicating that the diamond might not be what you think it is at first. Here are a few common red flags to be aware of:

- **Created or synthetic diamonds.** Some companies re-create in a laboratory the same conditions that cause a diamond to form in the earth, thus manufacturing synthetic, or lab-created, diamonds that have virtually the same properties as a diamond mined from the ground. These can potentially offer you a pretty diamond for a fair price, but because the process of "growing" the diamonds in a lab can be precarious and expensive, they're not plentiful and certainly not dirt-cheap. You should also know that many sellers on eBay inappropriately use the terms "created diamonds" or "synthetic diamonds" to describe cubic zirconia, or CZ—a synthetic, and relatively worthless, gemstone that's often referred to as an "artificial diamond." If your seller doesn't clarify what kind of created diamond he's selling, as in the auction shown in Figure 4.5, don't hesitate to e-mail to ask him before bidding.

- **Clarity-enhanced diamonds.** These are natural diamonds that, without enhancement, contain highly visible inclusions or fractures. The clarity-enhancement process involves coating these inclusions with a glass-like substance that contains refractive and optical properties similar to the diamond itself, making the inclusions invisible to the naked eye. Another option involves laser-drilling, or shooting a laser beam into the diamond to eliminate the inclusions.

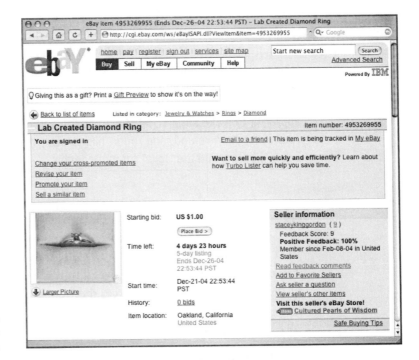

Figure 4.5

It's unclear from this auction description whether this diamond is a true lab-created diamond, with the same properties as a real diamond, or if it's simply a cubic zirconia fake diamond. E-mail the seller for clarification before bidding on auctions like this, especially if the price seems unbelievably low.

■ **Precarious settings.** A piece of beautiful diamond jewelry won't do you any good if the diamonds fall out! It never hurts to take any piece of jewelry to a reputable jewelry repair place once a year or so to have the prongs or setting checked for strength, but there are a few settings in particular with which you must take great care:

■ **Tension settings.** Avoid bidding on tension-set rings, which are rings that suspend a diamond between two pieces of metal and rely on the pressure and strength of the metal to hold the diamond in place. These kinds of rings must be manufactured precisely, or you'll lose the stone. You'll probably want to personally know the jeweler who sells this kind of ring to you.

■ **Invisible settings.** These involve square diamonds that are set side-by-side to create the look of a large area of diamond. This is another setting that, if not well-made, can put you in danger of losing the diamonds. Take care when purchasing invisible-set diamond jewelry at very low prices.

■ **Channel settings.** In these settings, round diamonds "float" beside each other in a row, held in place by a rim at the top and bottom of the channel. If the rims are not manufactured carefully, the diamonds can pop out.

■ **Retail prices.** Take any "suggested retail prices" with a grain of a salt. A diamond ring with a starting price of $1 would probably not really sell for $9,500 in a retail store, no matter how high the markup is in that store!

Colored Gemstone and Pearl Jewelry

Colored gemstones and pearls are often lumped into a single category in the jewelry trade, although there are countless varieties of both—hundreds of different gems that all come in many different colors and originate from different regions, affecting their hue, size, and quality.

Assessing the Quality of Colored Gemstones

Although they're not commonly associated with stones other than diamonds, the 4Cs can come in handy when shopping for colored gemstones too. That said, the grading scales for colored gems are much less formal. Color, while one of the most important determinations of a gemstone's quality, is often evaluated subjectively in terms of the hue of the stone. The color of a ruby, like the one shown in Figure 4.6, might be judged to be "very red," for instance. So much for the scientific, letter-based grades assigned to diamonds! Such a grading scale does not exist for colored gemstones quite simply because there are so many different kinds of gemstones that it would be impossible to build a color grading scale that worked for all of them. Unlike with diamonds, professionals pay close attention to the quality of the tone and saturation of the color for a colored gemstone. The richer and more spectacular the color, the more the stone is worth.

Similarly, clarity and carat weight are very important for colored gemstones, although the value associated with these characteristics might be harder to understand. Good cut is also very important, although color and clarity tend to take preference in grading quality. Colored gemstones still need to refract light, but don't need to do so as intensely as diamonds do in order to

Figure 4.6

A colored gemstone is graded based on the same 4Cs as a diamond, except that each C has its own considerations unique to a colored gem.

be beautiful. On the other hand, there do exist on the market poorly cut colored gemstones, which feature bad angles on the pavilion, or bottom, of the gem that prevent light from reflecting well and cause the gemstone to look dull. Cutters might purposely cut these gemstones that way to add weight to the stones, so they can earn a higher price for a bigger carat weight. These stones are called "windowed" because you can often see right through the top to the bottom of the stone.

Assessing the Quality of Cultured Pearls

Most of the pearls you'll find on today's market are *cultured pearls*, so called because most modern, commercial pearl development in oysters is initiated by humans and therefore can't be called "natural." Very rarely, you might run across real, natural pearls, especially in antique jewelry, but also occasionally sold as loose pearls or in modern jewelry. What's the difference? In nature, a pearl is formed when an intrusive particle such as a piece of shell becomes lodged inside a mollusk (often mistakenly called a pearl "oyster").

To protect itself, a mollusk begins coating the particle with *nacre*, a white, lustrous substance. Over time, the mollusk secretes enough of this substance to form a pearl. Unfortunately, these pearl mollusks have been overfished over many years, so it's rare to find real, natural pearls. The pearl trade instead cultures the growth of pearls by implanting beads in the mollusks and encouraging the growth of nacre.

As long as you look for good-quality cultured pearls, the fact that they are cultured should have no effect. That said, some purist collectors like natural pearls because they are made only of pearl nacre, whereas a cultured pearl is typically a few millimeters of nacre coating a shell bead (depending on the quality and variety of the cultured pearl, this coat of nacre can be very thin or very thick, but some people prefer the rare all-pearl option).

Shopping for cultured pearls is very different than shopping for colored gemstones, even though they're often grouped in the same category. Dealers do use a grading system (though not a universally recognized one, so grades can vary depending on the source), by which AAA is the best quality and C is low quality. The grades represent a combination of different quality factors in cultured pearls, which include the following:

- **Luster.** A pearl with great luster will have a sort of luminescence about it, an inner glow with a colorful sheen. Pearls with poor luster will appear flat, white, and even chalky. Good luster is the sign that the pearl is covered with a thick coat of nacre. Without sturdy nacre, your pearls could start to peel, leaving you with an ugly shell bead underneath.

- **Surface.** Almost all cultured pearls will have at least some very slight blemishes on them; those blemishes are how you can tell they're real pearls (as opposed to glass simulants), because they've spent time in the water and have been exposed to the wear of water and sand. That said, the less discernable the blemish, the more valuable the pearl. Very good quality pearls will have barely noticeable blemishes, while poorer quality pearls will show quite a few spots or cracks.

- **Shape.** The rounder the pearls, the more valuable they are. However, there are beautiful varieties of pearl shapes, including tear-shaped or drop-shaped, potato-shaped, and "baroque," or asymmetrical shapes, which are gorgeous and unique.

- **Color.** Depending on the variety, pearls can come in many different colors. Some colors are natural, and some are not. You should do a little research on the variety of pearl you plan to buy to find out what colors are possible.

- **Size.** Different from diamonds and colored gemstones, pearls are measured in size, not weight. Size is determined typically by the diameter of the roundest part of the pearl, measured in millimeters. Again, size ranges depend on the variety of pearl being measured. Some can start at 1 or 2 millimeters and only get as large as 5 or 6 millimeters, while others can grow as large as 20 millimeters. Bigger pearls are often more valuable, depending on other quality factors, of course.

There are several varieties of cultured pearls, each with its own unique set of characteristics. *Akoya* cultured pearls are the type most people think of when envisioning pearls. They're the small, white, round pearls you often see as strands. Traditionally they come from Japan, though they are also available from China. *South Sea* cultured pearls are the pearls you see movie stars and politicians wearing—huge, white or golden cultured pearls from Australia, Indonesia, and the Philippines. *Black* pearls (often known as *Tahitian pearls* because many of them originate in French Polynesia, of which the island of Tahiti is part) are also sizeable, but come in wild colors such as greenish gray and pinkish black. And *freshwater* pearls come in all shapes, sizes, and colors. Often farmed in the lakes and rivers of China (though some are produced in the United States and other countries), these pearls run the gamut between "rice krispie" shapes and large, round, beautiful forms, in a variety of gorgeous colors. While akoya, South Sea, and Tahitian are often pricey, freshwater pearls are often more affordable.

Buying with a Certificate

Certificates have become the standard with diamond selling, but they can also accompany very fine colored gemstones. If you're considering bidding on a piece that has a large and valuable center stone (such as a big ruby or sapphire), e-mail the seller to ask if she will provide a lab certificate proving the stone is natural and of good quality. It's rarer for cultured pearls to come with certificates, although some dealers are making pearl certification more of a habit these days.

Red Flags

Many of the red flags for gemstones and pearls are the same as for diamonds, although the details differ. Here are a few to look out for:

- **Synthetic gemstones.** Synthetics are more widespread with colored gemstones than with diamonds, just because the practice has been going on longer. As with diamonds, manufacturers simulate the formation of colored gemstones in a lab environment. You'll often see synthetics for more expensive and popular gemstones such as sapphires and rubies. Again, synthetics don't mean *fake*—they're real gemstones, with all the same properties. But because they're man-made instead of mined, you can get them at a better price—often without many of the flaws that come with natural stones. On the other hand, sellers are legally obligated to disclose whether a gemstone is natural or synthetic —it can affect the value of the gemstone and is important if you ever plan to re-sell the gemstone. Plus, many buyers who are drawn to the natural and miraculous beauty that colored gemstones offer might be disappointed to learn their gems were produced in a laboratory. So it's your right to know where your gemstone originated.

Note

The term *synthetic* may be misleading. Industry professionals use the term to mean lab-created, or man-made. Some sellers, however, might use it to mean *artificial*. Read the product description carefully. If the seller puts quotes around any terms, as in *2 CT. "RUBY"*, beware: You could receive a pretty, red piece of glass! When in doubt, e-mail the seller for clarification before bidding.

Note that there are no such things as synthetic pearls—that is, real pearls cultured in a lab. If you see a description for "man-made pearls," they're probably made out of glass, plastic, or shells, and are not true cultured pearls.

- **Gemstone and cultured pearl treatments.** Over the last couple decades, treatments, or enhancements, for colored gemstones and cultured pearls have become a major controversy. In truth, however, most cases of treated or enhanced gemstones or cultured pearls are not that big of a deal. Indeed, depending on the kind of gemstone you buy, you can assume it has been treated in some way. Because of the great demand for gemstones from around the world, they have been heavily mined, which means the naturally beautiful ones are fewer and farther between. With a few technological treatments, though, you can get a pretty emerald or ruby for less money than a non-enhanced one would cost you. Here's a look at some of the treatments you'll stumble across in the gemstone world.

■ **Heat treatments.** Gemstones are formed by cooling magma deep in the earth, and the color and other traits of a gemstone are determined by the elements that are hanging around in that magma as it crystallizes. Traders use heat treatments to change the structure of a gemstone so that the present elements "rearrange" themselves to produce an attractive color. Sapphires, such as the one in Figure 4.7, plus rubies, citrine, aquamarine, and tanzanite are almost always heat-treated to bring out their vivid colors. Some traders also use heat in rubies to remove imperfections.

Figure 4.7

Don't be alarmed if you learn your gemstone has been heat-treated; many of the most popular colored gems, such as sapphires, undergo exposure to intense heat to bring out their brilliant colors.

■ **Clarity enhancement.** Because colored gemstones are softer materials than diamonds, they often feature inclusions and fractures that buyers can see, thereby affecting the beauty of the stone. Gemstone traders have found a way to cover these fractures by injecting different kinds of materials into the stones—most commonly oils, resins, and glass. These treatments are most often found in emeralds and rubies; you can pretty much assume that lower-priced stones, especially, have received some kind of clarity enhancement. Oiled and filled stones require special care, so if you purchase a gemstone of a significant size, be sure to find a jewelry repair professional or gemologist who can help you care for your gemstone when you buy it.

■ **Irradiation.** As scary as it sounds, radiation is sometimes used to change the color of gemstones and cultured pearls; often, the treatment gives a gemstone an amazing makeover, changing it from one color to another completely. Radioactivity is dealt in relatively small doses, and traders who do use this method are legally required to hold on to the stones for an accepted period of time before releasing them to the public so the stones aren't dangerous. Unless the stone is exposed to extreme heat or light, the treatment is permanent. Stones that are commonly irradiated include blue topaz, smoky quartz, red tourmaline, and, occasionally, diamonds and pearls.

■ **Dyes.** You often see dyes used with cultured pearls. Dying is hard to spot, especially if it's used to pass off ugly pearls as pearls with pure white surfaces. More often, however, traders of inexpensive freshwater cultured pearls will dye their strands to sell them as colorful fashion accessories (see Figure 4.8 as an example). The problem is that dyes can fade or peel over time. Cultured pearls naturally come in subtle colors (and often have a sheen to them that suggests a rainbow of colors). If you see a photo in which the pearls appear to have an unnatural color (such as bright yellow, blue, or dark black), e-mail the seller and ask him whether the pearls have been dyed before bidding. Occasionally, you'll also find dyed gemstone beads—gemstones that have been rounded off as beads and strung rather than faceted and set in finished jewelry.

■ **Rough or uncut gemstones.** Just as the tabloids at the grocery checkout remind you constantly that movie stars look *terrible* without makeup, so now do you understand that all gemstones don't come out of the ground looking beautiful. And even if miners *do* uncover a perfect specimen, the stone might require hours or even days of careful cutting and polishing by professional gemstone cutters to make it desirable. A piece of *rough*, as an uncut gemstone is called, is typically no more attractive than a rock—or a pretty piece of quartz if you're lucky.

Figure 4.8

Metallic or bright, unnatural colors in cultured pearls often indicate they've been dyed or irradiated. E-mail the seller to ask. If the seller is obeying the rules, he will be straightforward with you about the processing to which the pearls have been exposed.

You'll see many listings on eBay, like the one in Figure 4.9, for lots of rough and uncut gemstones, which can be yours for very little money. Don't fall for it! It's somewhat difficult (thought not completely impossible) to walk into a corner jewelry store, hand over an uncut gemstone, and expect the jeweler to be able to cut and polish it. Only skilled cutters and faceters can do that kind of work—and the odds of finding one such faceter in your neighborhood gem shop or jewelry store are slim. Also, a rough gemstone for sale on eBay might not necessarily produce the most attractive cut and polished gemstone, even if you do find somebody to cut it for you. You might wind up with a cool paperweight and a fun story to go along with it—but probably little more.

Precious Metal Jewelry

Say you don't want to bother with gemstones at all—or maybe you do, but you care just as much about what they're set in as the stones themselves. You're smart: The metal used in jewelry can make or break the piece—literally! You want to make sure the metal is properly represented, or you could end up with a piece that scratches, tarnishes, peels, or breaks with minimal wear and tear.

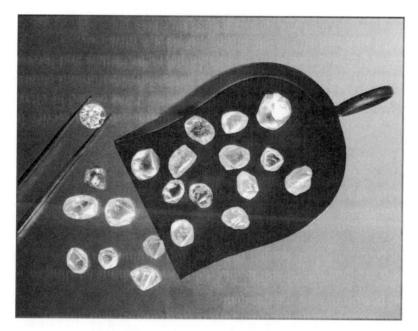

Figure 4.9

The lots of rough or uncut gemstones you'll see on eBay, similar to these uncut diamonds, sound romantic in theory, but they're really not so attractive in reality. If you're looking for a true beautiful gemstone, stick to the cut and polished ones.

Assessing Quality

Consumer laws closely regulate gold, platinum, and silver, the main "precious" metals in terms of what dealers are allowed to sell. These regulations ensure that sellers properly represent the purity and content of the metals. Gold, platinum, and silver used in jewelry are actually alloyed with other metals for color and hardness, so the metals are easier to manipulate when designing jewelry. With gold, the metal's purity is measured in *karats* (not to be confused with *carats*, for gemstones). For platinum and silver, laws regulate the metals according to the percentage that is pure platinum or silver.

Manufacturers who sell precious metal jewelry are required by law to sell the jewelry with a stamp, which is really an engraving in the metal, usually located on the underside of the piece. The stamp must include a hallmark—usually a symbol along with the manufacturer's name—and a measurement of the metal's purity. Here's what to look for with each metal:

■ **Gold.** The purest gold is 24 karats. In North America, gold is sold in several different increments, including 10 karats, 14 karats, 18 karats, 22 karats, and 24 karats. The higher the karatage, the softer the gold, because it isn't mixed with as many other metals. Therefore, it's harder to carve fine detail into higher-karat gold, but you get a richer yellow color. The karatage will be stamped as 10K, 14K, 18K, 22K, and 24K (though you rarely see 24-karat gold used in jewelry).

- **Platinum.** This hard, shiny white metal is available in North American markets at three quality levels: 95 percent, 90 percent, and 85 percent platinum. The marks will read 950 or PT950, 900 or PT900, and 850 or PT850. It's illegal to sell platinum marked any lower than 85 percent in the United States.

- **Silver.** The surest way to prevent that nasty green skin tone around your ring is to buy 95.8 percent or 92.5 percent silver jewelry (marked with .958 or .925). The 92.5 percent variety, known as sterling silver, is the most common.

Be sure that before you bid, the seller provides a picture of the jewelry's stamp. Many sellers will include such a photo with their description, but if a seller doesn't, contact him to see if he can e-mail a digital photo to you. Hold on to the photo and, if you win the auction, make sure it matches up with stamp on the jewelry you receive.

Red Flags

Buying precious metal jewelry ensures you'll have a piece that remains beautiful for years—an heirloom you can pass on to your children. But you must beware that you're getting what you think you are, or you could end up with jewelry that is overpriced and tarnishes or peels easily.

- **Underkarating.** There have been widespread problems with sellers—not just on eBay, but in many different channels—selling metal jewelry with stamps that misrepresent the actual karatage or purity of the metal, so be careful when purchasing gold and platinum jewelry that is priced extremely low for its karatage. Also, be sure the piece has a hallmark, or a mark with the manufacturer's name or logo, along with the purity mark. Misrepresented pieces often don't contain a manufacturer's hallmark, a sure sign of deception.

■ **Plating.** Plating has long been a way for people who want pretty jewelry to buy it, even if they can't afford the real thing. Here, gold is "plated" over a less expensive metal, providing the gold look without the price. However, plated gold will eventually wear away, so be sure you understand that if you are serious about buying a piece that lasts. Also note that plated pieces should not bear stamps.

Watches

Around 70 percent of all watches sold on eBay are brand new. Indeed, eBay is a great place to find a true bargain on a new watch. That said, watches are one of those categories that is plagued by counterfeiting. Have you ever been to New York City and seen the fake Rolexes for sale on Fifth Avenue? It's no better online, especially on eBay, which is why it's important to be aware of the danger and watch your step.

Assessing Quality

The inner workings of a watch can be a mystery to a buyer who doesn't understand the science behind watchmaking. That's why you must rely on a few true-blue guidelines to make sure you're buying something that will last.

■ **Brand name.** Watches, like the one shown in Figure 4.10, are different from other categories of jewelry because so much of the quality is inherent in the name of the manufacturer. In fact, from a quality standpoint, buying a watch is almost more like buying a car or a stereo than buying a diamond! You want to go with a name you trust. The other benefit of buying a well-known brand is that you have a better chance of getting a good manufacturer's warranty when buying from an eBay seller. If the watch is made by a manufacturer you've never heard of before, be sure to do a little digging on the Internet for information about that company before taking the plunge.

■ **Watch mechanisms.** How a watch works can play a big role in its value. You can choose from watches that are *mechanical*, or wind-up; *automatic*, or self-winding (usually fueled by the motion of the wearer's arm); and *quartz*, or battery-powered watches. Mechanical

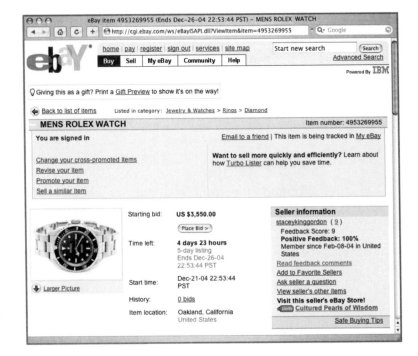

Figure 4.10

Sophisticated watches from international watch companies are in demand by collectors on eBay—and they can also be yours, most likely for a bargain.

and automatic watches use a tiny wheel and spring to keep time, while quartz watches use a tiny quartz crystal to maintain time. These mechanisms keep time by vibrating constantly. Quartz crystals tend to vibrate faster and more steadily, so quartz watches tend to keep time more accurately over a longer period. According to the American Watch Association, quartz watches tend to lose or gain no more than 10 seconds a month, while a mid-priced mechanical or automatic watch might lose around five or 10 minutes a month.

■ **Bells and whistles.** You can buy a watch that just tells time, or you can buy one that tracks the phases of the moon, the amount of distance you travel over time, the distance you're located from a train whistle or a clap of thunder, and a variety of different time zones, all on the face of your watch. These features, known as "complications" in the watch world, don't add to a watch's ability to tell time, but they are desirable additions for watch junkies, and can considerably increase the value of a watch.

■ **Durability.** You can find watches that can withstand water a few hundred feet below sea level, resist scratches, and keep on running through electric shock, magnetic fields, and dust storms. If you lead an active lifestyle, look for a watch that can stand the test of time.

■ **Materials.** Many watches are made of stainless steel, but if you're looking to spend more money, you can find solid gold watches or watches with diamonds. Keep in mind how you plan to wear the watch, of course, so your expensive gold watch doesn't end up with tons of scratches.

Red Flags

As with any category where brand names are hot, you have to make sure you're getting the real deal when you buy on eBay. And of course, you want to ensure your new timepiece will last.

■ **Counterfeits.** Unless you're a watch expert, it's very hard to tell the difference between an authentic watch and a counterfeit one, especially when a digital photograph is all you have to go by. Especially for watches that are infamous for being replicated with inexpensive fakes—brands such as Rolex, Omega, Tag Heuer, and Patek Philippe—pay close attention to the discrepancy between the price the watch is selling for and its actual retail price. Many thousands of dollars' difference can tell you a lot. Study the seller's returns policy, and be sure he or she promises a refund if it's determined that the watch isn't authentic. Also, read the seller's feedback carefully to see if there are any previous complaints from buyers about receiving fakes.

■ **Manufacturer's warranty.** If the watch is new, find out if it's covered under a manufacturer's warranty. If the seller purchased the watch from a closeout or liquidation sale, for example, a warranty might not be available. You're going to want to find out exactly how much coverage you have in case your watch stops working in the first year you own it.

Designer Jewelry

Many buyers like to shop for designer jewelry for a couple of reasons. First, there's a certain caché about owning a piece of jewelry with a recognizable style. It's a status symbol of sorts—others in the know spot your David Yurman necklace or Cartier bracelet and know you paid good money for it, just as if you were carrying a Coach bag, wearing a Burberry coat, or driving a Mercedes Benz sedan. In theory (although it's not a guarantee) you can feel confident that you're getting a good quality piece if a reputable design house puts its name behind it.

The big problem with buying designer jewelry on a site such as eBay is that you can't guarantee what you're getting is the real thing. Design houses control their distribution channels very closely. It's much less likely that a seller can get her hands on a ton of Tiffany & Co. jewelry during a liquidation sale than on nondesigner goods. Indeed, these days, it's getting harder to find authentic designer jewelry on eBay at all, especially from the big houses, simply because those companies have been waging war against online auction sites.

In June 2004, Tiffany & Co. filed a lawsuit against eBay stating that of the 186 items bearing the Tiffany & Co. hallmark that Tiffany had anonymously purchased and examined for authenticity, only 5 percent were really Tiffany items, while 73 percent were fake and were being passed off as the real deal. (The remaining 22 percent were labeled Tiffany, but in a way that suggested they were counterfeit—for example, with quotation marks around the name "Tiffany."

eBay addressed the issue by pulling about 19,000 auctions that appeared to falsely represent items as Tiffany hallmarks, but at press time the lawsuit remained active. This has translated to a serious downsizing in the number of designer pieces available on eBay; a recent search resulted in only about 1,600 items for the keyword **Tiffany**, a search that previously resulted in tens of thousands of hits.

Assessing Quality

When assessing the quality of a piece of designer jewelry, consider these points:

- **Designer name.** In the designer category, you've got several strata of offerings. The big guys you've heard of are backed by their priceless names: Tiffany, Cartier, Harry Winston, Van Cleef & Arpels. Then there are the modern superstars of designer jewelry, houses such as David Yurman, Lagos, and Penny Preville. Next are the designers who have "made it" because Hollywood stars have latched on to them—glitzy designers such as Me & Ro and Erica Courtney. There are also tons of designers who, although not known the world over, have developed a loyal following among jewelers and their customers. They might be rising stars, such as Ayiko Matsuoma and Jordan Schlanger, who have recently been picked up by exclusive department stores. They might be even smaller than that—designers of fine or fashion jewelry who are building a small but loyal following on eBay.

  So how does name equate with quality? Well, if they're smaller designers, they've most likely manufactured their jewelry by hand or with a cherry-picked production line, which suggests a high degree of craftsmanship. If they're larger design houses, they might be using factories, either in the United States or overseas, to manufacture their jewelry, but they probably have high quality standards. That's *not* to say that a designer piece is automatically better quality than an unbranded piece—that's not true at all. But you do know that there's some accountability, especially among prominent design houses, which in many cases will stand behind their pieces if something goes wrong (that is, assuming the jewelry isn't counterfeit).

- **Gemstones and metals used.** With designer jewelry, the same cause-and-effect relationship between valuable stones and metals and the price of the jewelry doesn't necessarily apply. For example, a Tiffany & Co. piece in sterling silver will, in the offline world at least, cost you much more than a similar piece made by a company with a less well-known name. Along the same lines, a hot design house might specialize in silver jewelry with semiprecious gemstones such as amethysts and topaz, and will charge a fortune for them even though the materials used aren't intrinsically wildly expensive. You pay for the name, of course. In cases such as these, you'll get more value from well-made, nondesigner jewelry that uses higher-quality materials.

Red Flags

Just like with brand names in any category of consumer goods around the world, designer jewelry is a popular target for knockoff artists. Be very careful as you shop for designer pieces on eBay, searching for warning signs and asking a lot of questions before placing a bid. Here are a few things to watch out for:

- **Counterfeits.** Some sellers who are auctioning true fakes will try to pass them off as the real thing. How can you tell, especially if the starting price for the auction is in the hundreds? Here are a few clues that things aren't what they seem:

  - **Private auctions.** Private auctions are those where the seller can hide the identities of the other bidders, as well as her eBay feedback. That means you can't see who's bidding against you, nor can you see what previous buyers have said about this seller. Although private auctions aren't inherently bad, they can be a sign that something's awry. Because bidders' IDs are withheld, other experienced eBayers can't e-mail them to warn them if something looks suspicious. Worse, your best weapon against fraudulent sellers—their feedback rating—has been hidden from you. If you suspect a piece might be counterfeit and the auction is private, you might want to move on to the next listing.

  - **A seller who is incommunicado.** You e-mail the seller your legitimate questions: How did you happen to acquire this Cartier watch? Do you offer any authenticity guarantees, such as a returns policy? If I cover your costs, could you have this piece authenticated before shipping it to me? The seller doesn't write back, or shoots you a terse reply but avoids answering your questions. Turn your back and walk away; this seller probably has something to hide.

- **Synonyms for "knock-off."** Auction houses and estate jewelry dealers for years have sold jewelry for years that, in their words, is "Tiffany style" or "inspired by Van Cleef & Arpels." This is the seller's friendly way of telling you that, yes, it is indeed a counterfeit, or at least a close replication, but that it has all the class of the authentic design. Look for clues in these auctions, such as the one in Figure 4.11, that serve as a wink and a nod to clue you in that the item isn't real.

(By the way, a seller is technically prohibited, according to eBay's rules, from using illegal comparisons such as "Tiffany style" in their listings. But many of them still do, and you should be aware what you're getting into when you bid on these listings.)

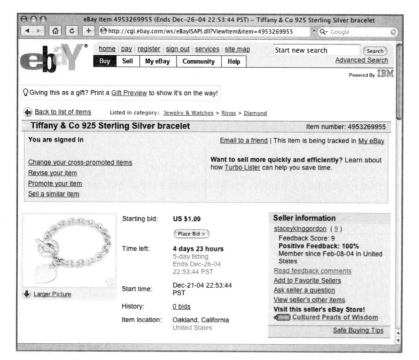

Figure 4.11

Is it or isn't it? Read the description carefully for clues about whether this is a counterfeit design.

Note

eBay tries to cut down on counterfeiting through the Verified Rights Owners (VeRO) program. Companies that own the rights to major trademarks (such as manufacturers, importers, and distributors), along with a dedicated team of eBay staff, scour the site to identify questionable listings and pull those auctions off the site. According to eBay, VeRO has gone a long way toward making counterfeiting less of a problem on eBay, so buyers can feel safer.

Estate and Antique Jewelry

Estate and antique jewelry (also known as vintage jewelry) can be challenging for a variety of reasons. For one thing, older jewelry was made with different standards, so the rules you've learned for newer jewelry may not apply. Older diamonds, for example, were cut differently and may not be as brilliant, but that doesn't necessarily make them less valuable. Another challenge is that, because the jewelry has presumably changed hands at least a few times through the generations, it's often difficult to tell what's original and what has been altered over the years.

Note

This category is much too complex to cover in a few short paragraphs. If you are genuinely interested in becoming a collector of valuable estate and antique jewelry, I suggest you find a book providing a good overview of the field, or better, one that goes into a lot of detail about the style you like.

Assessing Quality

Antique and estate jewelry play by somewhat different rules than modern-day pieces, simply because standards, rules, technology, and techniques were so different several decades ago than they are today (see Figure 4.12). Although buying vintage jewelry can be exciting and fun, you have to be familiar with what you're purchasing. Here are a few points to consider:

■ **Condition.** In the estate jewelry business, as with any antiques, dealers use lingo to describe the condition of a piece. Terms include *mint* or *near-mint* (like new), *excellent* (minimal wear, with no tarnishing or chips), *very good* (slightly visible wear, a few chips), *good* (more chipping and yellowing), and *fair* (missing stones and other visible damage).

■ **Pedigree.** Which would you rather have: a ruby brooch that's old, or an old ruby brooch that belonged to Queen Victoria's second cousin? If you're like the rest of us commoners, you probably will swoon for the piece with the romantic past. On the regular eBay site, pieces

Figure 4.12

Jewelry from popular design periods such as Art Nouveau can capture increased interest in buyers. If it's in exceptional shape and has a bit of allure attached to it, it can be even more sought after.

pre-owned by celebrities or royalty might be few and far between; the Sotheby's eBay site, on the other hand, is more likely to get consignments from the world's elite.

Red Flags

Here are a few pitfalls to avoid when it comes to antique and estate jewelry:

■ **Reproductions.** Some manufacturers do big business finding beautiful old pieces from in-demand jewelry periods—Art Deco, for example —and making close reproductions of them, so they look exactly like an older piece. There's nothing wrong with this in theory, unless a seller tries to pass it off as an estate piece. Be sure the seller sends you a picture of the hallmark and stamp before bidding. You will probably be able to tell from that information whether the piece is new or old. A resource such as *The Official Identification and Price Guide to Antique Jewelry* by Arthur Guy Kaplan (House of Collectibles, 1990) can help you check these hallmarks to determine age and authenticity.

■ **Inaccurate statements about period and pedigree.** Inexperienced sellers often make this mistake. If a piece *looks* like a Victorian necklace, the seller unequivocally *calls* it a Victorian necklace, even if the necklace was actually manufactured in Trenton, New Jersey, in the 1970s, not in England in the 1870s. Honest mistake, maybe, but it's a seller's responsibility to be accurate, even if it means being vague and not stating information definitively if he's not positive about it. Write to the seller to verify that he has proof that the piece has the background he says it does.

Fashion Jewelry

Shopping for costume, or fashion, jewelry is an entirely different animal from shopping for fine jewelry. You often don't need to pay much attention to gemstone authenticity, metal stamping, and the like. On the other hand, there's an entire market of avid collectors of fashion jewelry, especially vintage and designer jewelry, giving this category its own set of rules.

There are several types of fashion jewelry. The main kinds include the following:

■ **Vintage.** Signed, period costume jewelry, such as the brooch shown in Figure 4.13, is a hot collector's item, and can in some cases fetch prices comparable to fine jewelry.

Figure 4.13

Vintage costume jewelry is sometimes as competitive as fine estate jewelry, depending on the period and designer.

- **Designer.** Design houses such as Erwin Pearl create designs that mimic fashionable styles, using crystals and glass instead of gemstones.

- **Artisan.** Often using beautiful beads, these hand-crafted designs offer unique styles different from anything else you'll see in stores.

- **Replicas.** Some companies specialize in designing jewelry that looks exactly like a famous piece, such as a cultured pearl necklace worn by Jackie Kennedy.

Assessing Quality

There are no 4Cs of costume jewelry—quality and price tend to be based on, among other factors, the piece's craftsmanship and heritage. Here are a few points to consider when assessing quality of a fashion piece:

- **Craftsmanship.** A good piece of costume jewelry should be as lovingly crafted as fine jewelry, with earring posts and brooch backs that don't snap off, good polish, detailed filigree or carvings, and no visible glue or crooked edges that show the clumsiness of the work. Study the picture of the piece carefully, and if necessary, ask the seller to send more close-ups.

- **Likeness to fine jewelry.** This factor is important only if it's what you're going for. If you're seeking a pair of earrings that will fool your friends into believing you purchased real diamonds, look for auctions selling cubic zirconia or moissanite studs rather than rhinestone. E-mail the seller about how closely the stones resemble the real thing, and ask about getting your money back if you're not satisfied.

- **Materials.** Sometimes manufacturers will blend semiprecious stones or precious metals with artificial materials. Fine materials increase the value of the piece.

- **Designer name.** Especially in vintage costume collecting, pieces signed by certain designers are more coveted. Names you'll see include Weiss, Boucher, Miriam Haskell, Trifari, Hollycraft, Bogoff, and Eisenberg, among others.

- **Age and design period.** Vintage costume jewelry follows the same periods as fine estate jewelry, and the same popular periods are just as highly valued.

■ **Uniqueness.** If the piece is one-of-a-kind (or even 100-of-a-kind), its value will be much higher than if there are hundreds of thousands of them around the world. That's why determining whether the piece is original or a reproduction is very important.

Red Flags

Authenticity is the primary red flag, especially when it comes to vintage, artisan, or designer costume jewelry. Is the piece what the seller says it is, and how rare or unique is it? Especially with vintage costume jewelry, knockoffs are prevalent, and it's harder to spot them because a signature on a piece is less standardized than, say, a hallmark stamp on a piece of fine jewelry. Fortunately, there are tons of books on assessing the authenticity of vintage costume jewelry (refer to Chapter 2, "Doing Your Homework," for a partial list). Additionally, the Jewelry Collecting online forum on Delphi Forums (http://forums.delphiforums.com/jewelcol) features participants trading photographs of much-circulated fakes so they can spot potential problems.

chapter 5

Who's That Seller?

If Chapter 4, "The Ins and Outs of Jewelry Buying," taught you anything, it's probably that buying jewelry in general, and especially on eBay, is not for the faint of heart. Okay, so that's a little dramatic, but there *are* many things you need to watch out for. As I've said before, eBay is honestly no different from the offline world of buying and selling jewelry, except that you find yourself surrounded by thousands more pieces and thousands more sellers than you would in, say, a city jewelry district. From a purely statistical point of view, you're destined to run into a few bad apples from time to time.

On the other hand, it's safe to say that the *majority* of the sellers on eBay are honest. That's right—despite what you've heard (horror stories from co-workers or relatives) and read (blood-curdling tales that sell newspapers), this is a pretty solid marketplace. Is has to be; otherwise, eBay wouldn't have lasted a year, let alone gone on to become the most trusted e-commerce site on the planet.

"Trust is built by the sellers," says eBay Jewelry & Watches category manager Ann Poletti. And the sellers community knows that for the marketplace to succeed, it needs to stay consistently upstanding, which is why you'll often see sellers pointing out warning signs and bogus auctions in the eBay communities, such as the sellers' community shown in Figure 5.1. Behind the scenes, sellers often send e-mails to eBay pointing out auctions where something smells fishy. The sellers with integrity try to keep the block clean, so to speak.

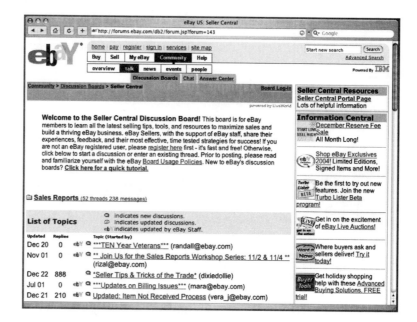

Figure 5.1

A tight sellers' community on eBay monitors and protects the integrity of the marketplace.

When shopping for jewelry and watches, assessing a seller's reputation and profile is absolutely critical to determining just what you're going to get. Combined with the shopping guidelines and red flags shared in the last chapter, a good solid portrait of who your seller is should put your mind at ease when you finally decide to place your bid. "You wouldn't just walk in and spent $5,000 at a retail store without checking out the storefront and the store's reputation," Poletti points out. Similarly, you'll want to familiarize yourself with the seller's history. This chapter shows you how to run your own little "background check."

Feedback

In each auction listing, you'll see the seller's user ID with a number listed beside it in parentheses. This number represents that seller's eBay feedback score. The number is a combination of feedback for both items sold and items bought, but it generally gives you an idea of how active the seller has been on eBay, how long he's been around on the site, and how credible he is.

The feedback score is calculated by tallying all of the user's positive, neutral, and negative feedback. A user receives one point for each positive comment and no points for a neutral comment. For each negative comment, one point is subtracted from the score.

In addition to viewing the seller's feedback score, you can also view actual feedback he or she has received. To do so, click the seller's user ID. At the top of the page you'll see a summary of the feedback received, tallying the number of positive, neutral, and negative feedback replies the seller has received in the past one month, six months, and year. But the most important number you'll see here is the percentage of positive feedback. You're looking for a very high percentage, roughly 97 to 98 percent or above. In the eBay world, anything lower spells trouble.

If the percentage of positive feedback seems high enough, but there appear to be a few negative marks on the seller's record, spend some time reading through the actual feedback comments, which are listed below the feedback score on the seller's feedback page. Are the positive ones unequivocally positive, or do you find that some of them are a little more reluctant? Do you detect a pattern among the negative complaints—buyer after buyer who commiserates about descriptions that don't accurately represent the items that arrive, or a seller's gross lack of communication? If in spite of a few negative comments the feedback seems overwhelmingly positive, with glowing remarks on quality, authenticity, fast shipping, flexibility with returns policies, and good communication, the seller appears to have earned a stellar reputation.

Note

Keep in mind that every once in a while a buyer and a seller don't see to eye-to-eye about something, which can launch an angry tit-for-tat of negative feedback. It's important to sort out these isolated incidents from a steady pattern of poor behavior.

Seller Symbols

In addition to displaying feedback information, eBay makes it a point to convey additional information about the seller in the form of icons beside the seller's user ID on the auction listing page and on the seller's listing page. They can tell you more about a seller than you might think:

- **PowerSeller.** A *PowerSeller* is an eBay seller who racks up a high volume of sales every month and maintains 98 percent positive feedback. A PowerSeller logo next to a seller's user ID, as shown in Figure 5.2, is a sure sign that you're dealing with an experienced, honest, and savvy seller. PowerSellers can attain one of five tiers:

- **Bronze:** $1,000 in sales each month

- **Silver:** $3,000 in sales each month

- **Gold:** $10,000 in sales each month

- **Platinum:** $25,000 in sales each month

- **Titanium:** $150,000 in sales each month

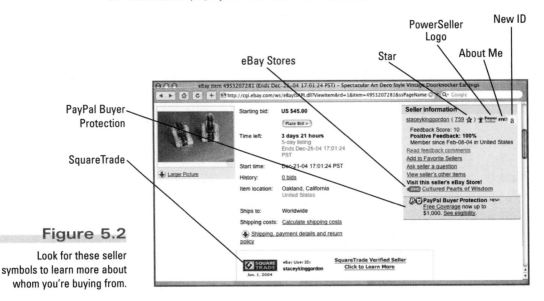

Figure 5.2

Look for these seller symbols to learn more about whom you're buying from.

- **Stars.** The star symbols on eBay represent the number of feedback ratings an eBay user has received. Experienced sellers will have shooting stars next to their user IDs, which symbolize thousands of feedback ratings and, thus, thousands of transactions—implying that the eBay member has a lot of experience. Depending on the level of experience, stars will appear in different colors, each color signifying a number of feedback ratings. Here's a list of star colors and the feedback score associated with each:

- **Yellow star:** 10–49 points

- **Blue star:** 50–99 points

- **Turquoise star:** 100–499 points

- **Purple star:** 500–999 points

- **Red star:** 1,000–4,999 points

- **Green star:** 5,000–9,999 points

- **Yellow shooting star:** 10,000–24,999 points

- **Turquoise shooting star:** 25,000–49,999 points

- **Purple shooting star:** 50,000–99,999 points

- **Red shooting star:** 100,000 or higher

- **eBay store.** It's reasonable to assume that sellers who set up eBay stores are here for the long haul. In order to having a minimum feedback score of 20, they must have invested the time required to build a broad catalog of items for sale. Plus, they're paying to be there. Spend some time browsing a user's eBay store by clicking on the icon next to the seller's user ID to see how many items she has for sale. Also study her sales history. Although this is not always true, you're most likely safer buying from somebody who has an established eBay store; that person has put down stakes and is less likely to take the money and run.

- **ME.** Each seller has the option to create her own About Me page, which provides buyers with additional information about the seller that isn't automatically provided by the feedback page. For example, a typical About Me page includes information about the seller's personal history, her business experience, her passion for jewelry (or what have you), and more. To access a seller's About Me page, click the seller's ME icon.

■ **New ID or Changed ID.** These icons alert you to the fact that the seller has another user ID registered on eBay or has recently changed his ID. Click the icons to check out the feedback for both the old and new IDs to make sure the seller isn't running from an ID with a lot of negative feedback.

■ **PayPal Buyer Protection.** Appearing just below the seller's information box on the auction listing page, this icon is important to watch for because it indicates that the seller supports the use of PayPal Buyer Protection. PayPal Buyer Protection gives a buyer the security of having up to $1,000 of insurance on her item if something bad happens—for example, if the item never arrives, or if it shows up damaged or breaks soon after it is received. Although offering this service costs the seller a small fee, it demonstrates that she stands behind her item, and that she cares about providing peace of mind to her buyers. Sellers must have a feedback score of 50 or higher and be a verified PayPal member to use the service.

■ **eBay Square Trade.** Sellers who post the Square Trade seal have committed to using the Square Trade Dispute Resolution service, a mediation service, if a dispute arises between you and the seller. Square Trade also gives you up to $250 in fraud protection when you buy from the member seller. All sellers who participate in Square Trade have had their identities verified by Square Trade.

Seller's History

What's this seller's story? Unless he discloses his real identity or links to his online store with a physical address and phone number, you don't know much about him other than the city, state, and country where he lives, and sometimes sellers don't even reveal that. Fortunately, however, you can learn more than you may think about what the seller *knows*, which is what really matters anyway.

While you're looking at the seller's feedback, start drilling down into the products he's been selling. In the right-hand column next to each feedback listing, click the linked item numbers. In this way, you can see all the seller's auction listings and item descriptions from the previous six months, as shown in Figure 5.3. It's especially insightful to skip back to the very old listings. What you're looking for here is a sense of whether the seller has been specializing in jewelry and watches for awhile, or if this is a fly-by-night endeavor for him. If his previous listings run more to gardening tools, used blue jeans, bowling shoes, or vintage pottery, this might not be a seller who knows exactly what he's selling.

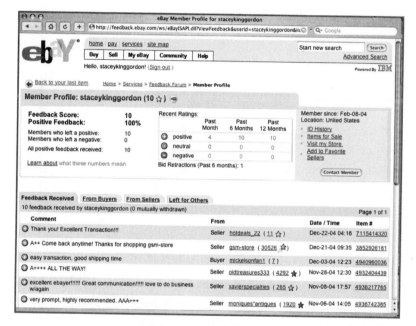

Figure 5.3

Drill down into a seller's history to learn whether jewelry and watches are a new hobby or a long-time specialization for him.

Item Description

You can tell a lot about a seller from the way she writes an item description, such as the one shown in Figure 5.4. A neat, classy, attractive item description tells you a lot about how savvy the seller is, which can give you a good idea about whether you're dealing with an upstanding merchant. To get a fix on whether the seller of an item that interests you is on the up and up, read through the item description and ask yourself the following questions:

- Is it well written?

- Are there quite a few typos?

■ Does the seller appear to have spent some time making the description sound good, or does she seem to have been in a big hurry?

■ Are the photos blurry and poorly lit, or has the seller tried to post the photo with the most detail?

Figure 5.4

It's important to study an auction description to see how knowledgeable and careful a seller is with each of her items, as well as how clear and upfront she is being to her potential buyers.

In short, the listing content should be detailed, not vague. On the other hand, you want to make sure the seller's not using trendy buzzwords to get hits on her listing, while not accurately representing the item.

Sales Policies

Study your seller's policies—usually located at the bottom of an auction listing, such as in Figure 5.5—to see how adamantly he stands behind his merchandise. Determine the following:

■ Does he offer a money-back guarantee if the item doesn't arrive exactly as described?

■ Does he accept PayPal or other secure forms of payment?

■ Will he offer insurance on shipping?

■ Is what he's charging for shipping reasonable for what you're buying? An honest seller will prove his integrity with fair shipping policies.

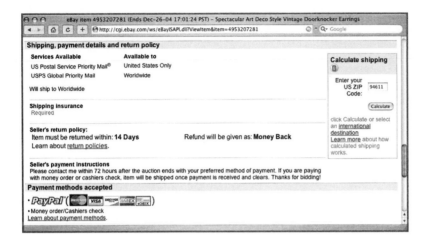

Figure 5.5

Scroll to the bottom of the page to carefully read a seller's sales policies, so you won't have any surprises after the auction is over.

If you're feeling safe about the seller from whom you're buying, you can feel safe about the item. A seller who covers all the bases has most likely gone to the same lengths to make sure the items he or she is selling are authentically and honestly represented.

chapter 6

When, and How, to Bid

Performing your background research may have been time-consuming and—let's face it—maybe even a little boring compared to the thrills you expected from eBay when you first arrived here. But trust me when I tell you that you won't be sorry for setting that foundation, especially when you complete that first sale. And now, at long last, you get to do what you came here to do: start bidding on jewelry items.

Are You Ready?

At some point, you have to stop preparing and just take the plunge. You know you're ready to start bidding if:

- **You've set goals for yourself.** You have established a price range based on the research you've done, you are confident about why you're buying the piece and how you want to use it, and you're realistic about your limitations, both on price and on what qualities you're willing (or, as the case may be, unwilling) to compromise.

- **You have at least a basic understanding of what you're bidding on.** You know the characteristics that define quality for the type of jewelry you want, and you understand the pitfalls on eBay well enough to detect and avoid them. Put another way, you can read an auction description, like the one shown in Figure 6.1, and understand what you're getting into.

■ **You comprehend, and are able to take, the risk.** At the end of the day, the overarching philosophy of eBay is *buyer beware*. You now understand the landscape well enough to watch out for yourself, but—just like in any risky proposition, from playing the stock market to buying real estate—there's always the distinct possibility you're going to lose your shirt. You have to be OK with that slight possibility before placing your first bid.

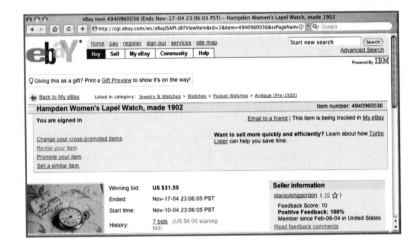

Figure 6.1

Do you understand what you'll be getting when you see the description for this item? If not, you may need to do a little more research before you start bidding.

A Bid Is a Contract

A bid is a contract. You'll see this phrase again when you're ready to place your first bid, but it's a good mantra to repeat to yourself. It means that, except under extenuating circumstances, you don't have a chance to change your mind after you bid. Even if the auction won't be over for five more days, you're committed to paying the price you bid if you win the auction. Your car could break down, your basement could flood, you might need to flee the country—but you're still obligated to pay what you promised to pay if you're the highest bidder.

eBay is a site that inspires impulse. I can't tell you how many times I've bid on something that seemed pretty or cool, only to find myself crossing my fingers an hour or two later that someone would outbid me. I watched the auction with trepidation, and if I won, I paid reluctantly. Part of the reward of eBay is the thrill of the competition, and the excitement of watching your mailbox every day waiting for your precious new treasure to arrive. Buyer's remorse is no fun at all, but bidder's remorse is even worse—because even though you know immediately you've made a mistake, there's absolutely nothing you can do about it even if you haven't secured the item yet.

Note

What if you suffer one of those foolish moments, bid on an item, then later decide you don't want it? What's to stop you from just never contacting the seller and walking away? The eBay community has provisions to punish that kind of behavior. A seller can file an unpaid item claim, and eBay will inflict a "strike" against your account. If you receive three strikes in a certain period of time, eBay will suspend your account. In addition, you'll probably receive negative feedback from the seller, which is detrimental to your eBay career. If you do realize after you've placed a bid that you can't or don't want to go through with the sale, you can e-mail the seller and ask if he would be at all amenable to allowing you to cancel your bid. A seller is under no obligation to let you do that, of course, but some sellers might be okay with it, especially if the auction is active with many other bidders.

So do consider your bid very carefully before clicking that Confirm Bid button. Walk away for a little while. Weigh your options carefully. Is this item something you need or have been wanting for some time? Have you shopped around to see what else is out there? Do you have the cash or can you justify running up your credit card to pay for this item? Only when you've checked your impulse and decided you're making the right decision should you return to your computer and place that bid.

Note

Although a bid is a contract, there are a handful of circumstances in which you are allowed to retract bids. These are discussed in the section "Retracting Bids" later in this chapter.

Using the Watch List

If you think you *might* like to bid on the item but aren't quite sure yet, you can put the auction on your watch list. If you are signed in, click the Watch This Item link, located on the upper-right section of the page below the item number. Now, and until the auction ends, every time you sign in and visit your My eBay page, you'll see a mini-listing of that item with the product description, current bid, number of bidders, time left for the auction, and seller's name (see Figure 6.2). If you decide to take the plunge and bid on the item, you can do so directly from the My eBay page.

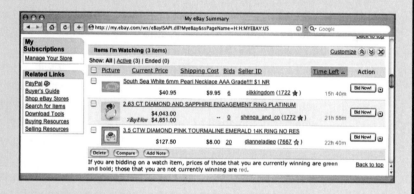

Figure 6.2

Using Watch This Item in My eBay is a convenient way to keep tabs on an item without actually committing to it.

Reading the Terms of Sale

Beyond the essential rule of treating a bid as a contract, you are subscribing to an individual seller's rules when you bid on an auction. You'll find these sales policies listed at the bottom of each auction listing, and even occasionally in the item description itself. For example, a seller might specify that:

- She expects the winning buyer to contact her within 24 hours.

- She will only accept money orders—no PayPal, credit cards, or personal checks.

- She won't ship outside of the United States.

- She'll only ship via standard mail—no courier services or express mail—so you won't be able to track your package.

- She ships items about 30 days after you win them, so you're required to wait awhile.

Most sellers are more laid back than the one I invented here, and won't list such strict contingencies. But some do, and if you don't read an auction's terms of sale carefully, you might be in for a rude awakening. Say you're buying a bracelet for your sister's birthday, which is coming up in 15 days, but your seller takes four weeks to ship items out, then uses standard, first-class U.S. Postal Service mail to send the item. You could be waiting for a month and a half for your item to arrive, and your sister will never receive her birthday gift in time. As the buyer, you are obligated to read and abide by these terms, even if you think they're unreasonable. If you don't like the terms, don't place a bid.

When Not to Bid

There are definitely instances when you need to trust your instincts, resist your impulse, and walk away from bidding. You should refrain for bidding for an item if:

- An item description is not clear, it uses terminology you don't quite understand, or the picture of the item doesn't seem to match the written description of the item.

- You have e-mailed the seller with questions, and you either don't hear back or you receive vague or curt answers in reply.

- You can't comply with, or aren't prepared to abide by, the shipping terms the seller has set.

- The seller's feedback shows quite a few negative scores, or many of the comments in the feedback suggest that expectations weren't met even if the feedback was positive.

- You strongly suspect the item is counterfeit.

- The seller appears to be hiding something—his feedback, his where-abouts, or other vital information.

Bidding Basics

Once you've determined you're comfortable with the item description, seller's reputation, and terms of sale, you're ready to place a bid. The first thing you want to do is to survey the scene:

1. Check out the bidding situation thus far. What is the current bid price, and how many bidders are vying for the item?

2. Click Bid History to see who the other bidders are, and how quickly the price has climbed.

3. Return to the auction listing and note when the auction is closing.

4. Search for similar items that have already sold to see what price they fetched. For details on searching for completed auctions, see the section "Researching an Auction" in Chapter 2, "Doing Your Homework."

These basic pieces of information will help you determine how in-demand an item is, as well as just how high the price might climb. An item that's already risen dramatically in price and still has three days of bidding left could fetch a handsome sum—and be less of a deal for you.

Pricing Options

Generally, a seller can choose to set up an auction with three different pricing structures:

- **No starting price.** Also known as "$1 minimum" or "no reserve" auctions, these auctions start at a bid price of zero and incrementally rise as buyers place bids.

- **Starting price.** The seller has set a minimum price where the bidding must start, typically to protect her investment so she at least makes her money back or earns a bit of a profit. Your bid must be above this starting price, and bids will climb from there.

- **Reserve.** The seller has established a price below which he will not sell the item, but this price is not published for bidders to see (see Figure 6.3). The price continues to climb incrementally as buyers bid, but it might not cross the reserve threshold. If bidding fails to meet the reserve price, the item does not sell and the seller can re-list it for auction. The purpose of the reserve is to drive bidding—buyers are competing against themselves, but also against the secret reserve price.

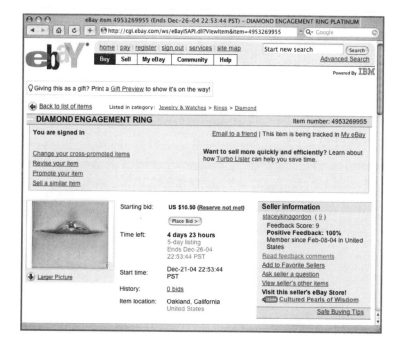

Figure 6.3

An item that has a reserve price will sell to the highest bidder only if the sale price reaches the reserve threshold.

Dutch Auctions and Live Auctions

From time to time you'll see other kinds of auctions that have different rules. One of these is a Dutch auction or multiple item auction, in which the seller has several identical items for sale. In a Dutch auction, buyers place bids that include both the price they want to pay and the quantity they want to buy. The people who bid the highest prices are guaranteed the quantities they want first, followed by lower bidders on a first-come, first-served basis. But the final price is the lowest successful bid—that is, the lowest bid placed by a winning bidder. This is a bit confusing; luckily, you don't run across them that much. For a lengthier explanation of Dutch auctions, visit http://pages.ebay.com/help/basics/g-dutch-auction.html.

The other kind of auction you'll see is a live auction. These are auctions held by old-school auction houses; you actually bid against other buyers for an item in real time during a scheduled auction session. Alternatively, you can enter an absentee bid before the auction starts if you can't be there at the time it starts. You'll have to sign up to participate before you can bid.

Placing a Bid

Regardless of whether you're bidding on a no starting price auction, a starting price auction, or a reserve auction, placing your first bid is easy. Simply click Place Bid on the auction listing page. On the bid page (see Figure 6.4), enter the *maximum* price you're willing to pay. For example, if the highest bid is currently $75 but you're willing to pay up to $125 to win the item, type **125**. Click Continue, and then review your bid and click Confirm Bid. When you do, eBay will automatically bid for you in increments all the way up to your maximum bid price.

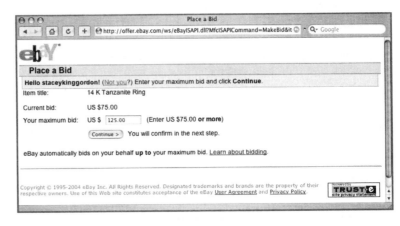

Figure 6.4

Enter your maximum bid and click Bid Now. You'll only pay the price necessary to outbid other buyers, so even if your maximum bid is high, you might pay much less.

The increments by which your bid will be automatically raised depend on the price of the item, as shown in Table 6.1. In the preceding example, if the current bid is $75 and you bid $125 as your maximum bid, the current bid will jump to $76, with you as the highest bidder. If a competing bidder has entered a maximum bid of $80, the system will automatically counter with your bid of $81. If nobody bids against you at that price, then the item is yours for $81, but the system will continue countering on your behalf all the way to $125.

If another bidder has already entered a maximum bid that's higher than yours, you will receive a message instructing you to bid higher. If you're willing to pay more, try entering maximum bids in increments of $5 above your original bid until you no longer receive the error message. Other bidders can't see what your maximum bid is, so nobody else knows how high you're willing to go.

Table 6.1 Bid Increments

Current Price	Bid Increment
$0.01-$0.99	$0.05
$1–$4.99	$0.25
$5–$24.99	$0.50
$25–$99.99	$1
$100–$249.99	$2.50
$250–$499.99	$5
$500–$999.99	$10
$1,000–$2,499.99	$25
$2,500–$4,999.99	$50
$5,000 and up	$100

Keeping Track of Your Bids

You can use My eBay to manage and watch all the items on which you're bidding, as shown in Figure 6.5. Once you're signed in, access your My eBay page by clicking the My eBay tab; then click Bidding on the left menu. The Bidding page will tally the number of items on which you're bidding, the number of auctions you're currently winning, and the total amount you're currently bidding.

If another buyer outbids you, eBay will automatically send you a notification by e-mail. However, if you're not keeping your eye on the auction and the closing time for the auction is approaching, this e-mail notification might come too late. If you're serious about winning, try the bidding strategies outlined next.

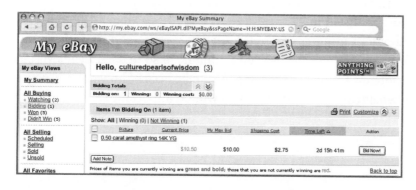

Figure 6.5

Use My eBay as an easy dashboard for managing all the items you're bidding on and watching.

Bidding Strategies

Yes, there *is* a science to successful buying on eBay, and eBayers who have been around for awhile know it. Unlike your typical impulse buy, just because you spot the cuff links you've been waiting for all your life doesn't mean that placing a bid will secure them for you. You have to stay invested throughout the length of the auction, or your cuff links could end up in a savvier bidder's hands.

Sniping: Saving the Best for Last

The most common strategy for winning an eBay auction is known as *sniping*. Sniping means waiting until just before the auction ends to place your bid, taking other bidders by surprise and snatching the item up at the last minute. The term makes it sound like a sneaky practice, but some eBay vets use the technique regularly to win items—for a few very good reasons:

- It prevents the price from being jacked up over several days through competitive bidding.

- It allows you to watch an item's performance and judge its desirability and market potential (especially if you're planning to resell it) before you bid.

- It gives you a better shot at outsmarting the competition.

Succeeding at Sniping

If you're really interested in an item, click Watch This Item to put it on your watch list, and note the end time of the auction on your calendar. (Make sure end times are listed in your time zone, and if they aren't, take that into account!) About 15 minutes before the auction is set to end, start watching the bidding action. Refresh the page every minute or so to see if there's visible last-minute interest from other bidders. Also take note of how quickly pages are loading when you refresh them—this will be important later.

Your next steps are avowed by eBay bidding experts as a sure way to win:

1. As the minutes tick away, open two different browser windows. In window number one, navigate to the auction listing. In window number two, open the auction listing again, then click Bid Now to set your browser to the Bid screen (see Figure 6.6).

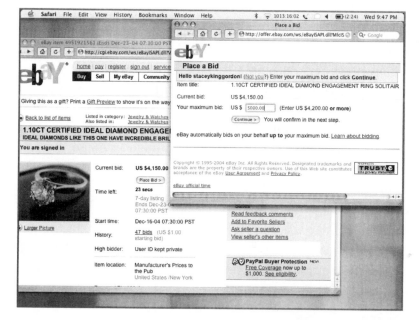

Figure 6.6

Submitting a last-second bid—a practice known as *sniping*—can be risky business, but it can also help you steal an auction without running up the price.

2. In the last few minutes of the auction, continue refreshing the auction listing in window number one to see the current price. Refresh once about every 10 seconds or so to see the latest price increase and the updated time left.

3. When there are about 15 seconds left for the auction, switch to your second window. Based on the latest price, enter your high bid.

4. Check window one a final time by refreshing the window. Then move to window number two, verify your high bid, click Bid Now, and then click Submit on the review page.

5. The auction is now over. Return to the first window and refresh it to see if your sniping paid off. If it did, your user ID will appear next to the label Winning Bidder.

Sniping Tools

Performing this song and dance with the multiple browser windows might be a tried-and-true method—but who has the time to do it every time? If you're bidding on several items at once, do you really want to be around every time one of them is ending to swoop in and handle the precarious task of last-minute bidding?

Luckily for you, there are dozens of sniping software and services on the market to help you with automatic sniping. Brands include eSnipe (see Figure 6.7), Power Snipe, AuctionStealer, SnipeRight, ISnipeIt, and Auction Sentry. Some are Web sites that you register to use, while others are software packages that you download to your PC. Most of them involve a small, one-time fee, which successful buyers testify is worth it. If you become a regular buyer and sniping is part of your secret for success, you might want to consider one of these packages.

Figure 6.7

Services such as eSnipe allow you to place a bid and then let the software place a snipe bid automatically in the final seconds of an auction.

Alternatives to Sniping

Even though it is technically legal, many eBayers—buyers and sellers alike —are outraged by the practice of sniping. They feel like it's dishonest and unfair—that buyers should engage in an honest bidding challenge with other buyers, true to the traditional auction format. Sellers also might resent that perhaps they didn't earn a final selling price that appropriately represented the level of demand for the item, because the "sniper" refused to participate in the bidding process.

To snipe or not to snipe is a personal decision. Especially if you're a buyer who has been outdone by a sniper, or a seller who feels he's been cheated out of good deal by a sniper, you might strongly oppose the practice. Indeed, many eBayers speak out adamantly against sniping on the community boards. Depending on your take on the matter, you might want to use other bidding strategies that are tamer, but equally effective. These techniques include

- **Lowballing.** This involves placing a bid that is only slightly higher than the highest bid—enough to remain in the lead, without risking paying too much. You can either bid in minimum increments, or you can raise the bid by several dollars to gain a little more of an edge. Of course, this requires you to be very vigilant about watching an auction to ensure that you don't get outbid.

- **Proxy bidding.** Decide how much you're comfortable paying, and place that high bid one time—letting the eBay system automatically bid on your behalf as normal. Of course, the trick here is deciding how much you're comfortable paying. To get a ballpark figure, research the average prices for which similar items have recently sold, and then place a proxy bid that's 10 or 15 percent above that price.

Retracting Bids

There are a handful of circumstances in which you are allowed to retract bids. For example, if you made a typographical error and entered the wrong bid amount, you can retract the bid, but you must immediately enter the new bid with the amount you meant to type. If you don't re-enter a bid right away, your account could be suspended. Other instances where you could retract a bid legally are

- If the seller significantly changes the description of the item after you bid on it

■ If you have tried to phone or e-mail the seller and are receiving messages indicating the phone number is out of service or the e-mail account has been closed—suggesting your seller might take your money and run

■ If somebody has hijacked your user ID and password and placed a bid without your knowledge

eBay investigates all bid retractions, so be sure you are within legal boundaries before retracting a bid. To retract a bid, do the following:

1. Go to http://pages.ebay.com/help/buy/questions/retract-bid.html and click the Bid Retraction form at the bottom of the page.

2. On the Bid Retraction form, shown in Figure 6.8, enter the auction number in the Item number of auction in question field.

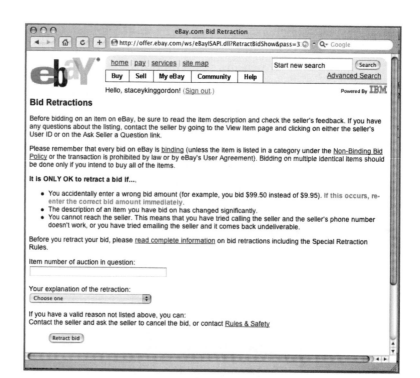

Figure 6.8

If you must retract your bid and you meet any of the criteria for legally doing so, you should use the Bid Retraction form to submit your retraction.

3. Select the reason for your bid retraction from the pull-down menu. Possible reasons include

   ■ Entered wrong bid amount

   ■ Seller changed the description of the item

   ■ Cannot contact the seller

4. Click Retract bid.

Buy It Now Instead of Bidding

Some sellers offer the option to "Buy It Now" rather than waiting for the auction to be over. The Buy It Now price will be higher than the current bid price, but the idea is that you automatically "win" the item for a flat price, which is in theory still a bargain. If you find a piece you can't live without, Buy It Now will guarantee that you win the item—although you may pay a premium price for that guarantee. If a seller offers the Buy It Now option, the Buy It Now price will be listed alongside a But It Now icon on the auction listing page, as well as next to the item in the category list or in the search results.

In the case of an auction, the Buy It Now option is only available to you if no bid has been placed. Once somebody places a bid, the Buy It Now button will disappear from the auction listing page, and the auction proceeds as usual. Buy It Now is an attractive option if you want to end the auction fast and get the item in your hands quickly—for example, if you're buying a gift or an item for an imminent occasion. Some sellers, however, bypass the auction format entirely. That is, you don't have the option of bidding on the item, but instead must buy it at the listed price. In such cases, sellers have chosen to sell the item at a fixed price, often because they are selling the item in their eBay store or because they have multiple quantities of the same item and wish to sell them at set prices.

To use the Buy It Now feature to purchase an item, do the following:

1. Check to see if the seller is offering the Buy It Now option by checking the auction listing page. If the item is being sold as an auction and no bids have been placed, or if a seller is using a fixed-price format rather than an auction format, the Buy It Now option will appear.

2. Click Buy It Now.

3. Review the purchase price and shipping and handling charges. Then click Commit to Buy, as shown in Figure 6.9.

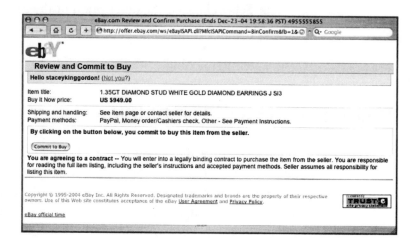

Figure 6.9

If you've found the item of your dreams and can't wait several days and risk losing the auction, you can use the Buy It Now feature, if offered, to secure the item.

chapter 7

What Happens If You Win?

So your patience paid off! You pounced with the right bid at the right moment, and the item is yours. Victory is sweet, and it's normal to gloat a little, especially if you won despite a fierce bidding war with other buyers. Winning on eBay never seems to lose its novelty. No matter how many times you come out on top, seeing your user ID in lights next to the word "Winner" is, well, very sweet. But now you face a phase of the buying process that can become disheartening if you're not ready for it. You have to secure the item by paying for it—and then the long wait begins.

Communicating with Your Seller

The first thing that will happen after you win your auction is that you'll receive an automated e-mail message from eBay, informing you that you've won the item (see Figure 7.1). The e-mail will show you the final sales price and provide you with links so you can quickly get to the site, pay, and register feedback, when you're ready. Don't do anything just yet. You should receive an e-mail communication from your seller soon, probably within 24 to 48 hours. Unless you corresponded with the seller before bidding to ask questions, this will be the first time you've interacted with the seller directly.

Sellers handle this part of the sale differently depending on their setup and preferences. Some, especially larger companies, will send you a canned e-mail requesting payment within a certain period of time, but they don't want any correspondence from you other than a timely completion of the transaction.

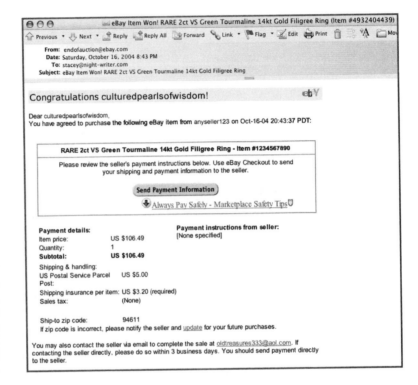

Figure 7.1

You will receive an e-mail from eBay after you win an auction. Afterward, you should receive a communication directly from the seller, either a personal message or a templated e-mail instructing you how to pay.

Others, especially individual sellers, will send more personal e-mails, and will ask for an e-mail back from you to touch base.

This e-mail from your seller should cover the terms of sale, including the seller's shipping cost and policy, and her accepted forms of payment. If you read the auction carefully before bidding, this shouldn't be any surprise to you. The main thing you'll need to communicate back to the seller is how you plan to pay—by PayPal or some other method. Sellers' terms vary on what they expect if you use a different form of payment, such as personal check or money order.

It's important to follow sellers' directions and comply with their instructions in a timely manner. Some sellers will actually stipulate that, unless they hear from you within 24 hours of the first e-mail, they'll repost the item in a new auction. Other sellers get extremely nervous if you don't write back right away—and rightly so, because many of them fall victim to buyers who disappear after winning an auction. So be on the lookout for this correspondence, and give your seller the courtesy of a timely reply.

Checking Out

To pay for your auction, do the following:

1. Log in to your eBay account and click My eBay.

2. In the left menu bar are links with numbers beside them in parentheses: Watching, Bidding, Won, and Didn't Win. The number beside the Won link should be one higher than before you won this new auction. Click Won.

3. On this page, shown in Figure 7.2, you'll see a listing of all the items you've won in recent history. The listing summarizes the seller ID, item description, item number, sale price, and other information. Review this information to make sure it matches with what you expected.

Figure 7.2

When you go to My eBay after you win an auction, you'll see a review of all the items you've won. From here, you can click Pay Now to check out.

4. Under Action, you'll see a link or a button that tells you what you need to do next. At this point, you're ready to pay, so the button will instruct you to pay now. Click this button.

5. The next page instructs you to review your purchase. Here you'll see your final sales price, including shipping and handling costs and any additional charges or discounts. The seller's payment instructions will also be posted here. Review all of this carefully.

6. At the bottom of the page, you will be asked to select one of five radio buttons beside desired forms of payment. At the top is PayPal, which, if you've already set up a PayPal account, will be your easiest and fastest way to pay. Other forms of payment include money order, personal check, credit card paid directly to the seller, and "other."

7. If you select PayPal, click Continue and you'll be automatically rerouted to the PayPal login page. Once you log in, the PayPal payment form will be prepopulated with the seller's information and the amount due for the item. Simply review the information and click Pay Now. If you decide to use another form of payment, select the radio button beside the form of payment you want to use, then click Continue. You will be directed to a form that automatically includes a short message to your seller about how you plan to pay, the item number, and the sale price (see Figure 7.3). The form allows you to add your own message of up to 500 characters in case you want to notify your seller about when you're sending your check or money order, or how you plan to send your credit-card information. Check your shipping details and make note of the address to which you should send a check or money order. Then click Send Information to Seller.

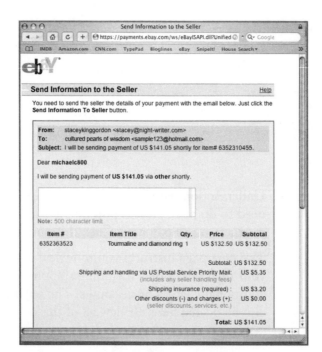

Figure 7.3

If you're not using PayPal to pay, you can submit a message to your seller informing him how you plan to pay.

After you've completed step 7, your account will be marked "paid" in the eBay system. If you elect to pay using a method other than PayPal, it will be up to you to work out the payment details with the seller directly.

Using Other Forms of Payment

Although PayPal is the most popular form of payment among buyers and sellers, sometimes it's not an option—either because a seller doesn't accept it, or because it's not feasible for you as a buyer. Of the other options available, some are more desirable than others:

■ Personal or cashier's checks and money orders are traceable to the address to which you mail them, are covered under eBay's purchase protection program, and often can be stopped before the payment goes through to protect you. You can use a service such as BidPay (http://www.bidpay.com), shown in Figure 7.4, to electronically request a money order, which the service will mail to your seller.

■ On the other hand, bank-to-bank wire transfers and cash wire transfers (such as the type available through Western Union), which move your money directly into the seller's bank account, *can't* be traced in case of fraud.

Figure 7.4

BidPay is a convenient, and easily traceable, way to send money orders to sellers who don't accept PayPal.

■ Another option is escrow. An escrow service holds on to your money until you receive and inspect the item from the seller, and then sends the money along to the seller. Although this is an attractive option for items priced over $500, be aware that there are some illegitimate escrow services out there. Escrow.com (http://www.escrow.com) is eBay's approved service.

Hurry Up and Wait

After you've sent your payment, you should receive an e-mail from the seller within a day or two notifying you that he has received your payment and letting you know when the item will ship. If you don't hear from your seller in 48 hours, send him an e-mail to touch base and ask when the item will ship.

Unless the seller's terms stated otherwise on the auction listing, you should expect to hear that the item will be packed up and shipped to you within several days after the auction ends. Buyers who pay promptly should anticipate sellers who reciprocate with quick shipping. However, depending on the form of shipment a seller selects, you might still have to wait a couple of weeks to receive your item. Be patient, and if possible secure a tracking number from the seller if he sends it by courier or U.S. Postal Service Priority Mail, Express Mail, or Registered Mail so you can make sure the item is on its way. To use the U.S. Postal Service's Web site to track the package, do the following:

1. Go to http://www.usps.gov, the U.S. Postal Service's Web site.

2. Click Track & Confirm in the top navigation bar to open the page shown in Figure 7.5.

3. Enter your entire tracking number in the Enter Label Number field and click Go.

4. The tracking page will show you the current status of your package. Click Shipment Details to view where your package has been throughout its journey, as shown in Figure 7.6.

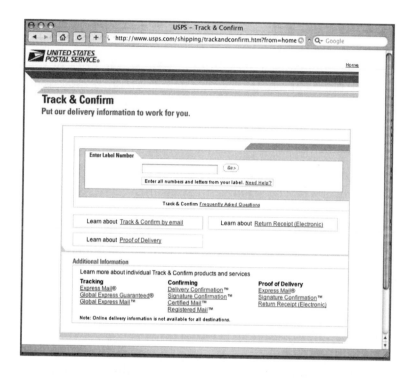

Figure 7.5

Be sure to get your item's shipping tracking number so you can keep tabs on where it is as it makes its way to you.

Figure 7.6

The U.S. Postal Service's Web site will show you the complete history of your package, to let you know where it is in its long journey from your seller's home to yours.

Insurance

Sometimes, sellers will automatically tack insurance on to the price of the shipping, especially if a piece of jewelry is very valuable. In other cases, sellers will not claim responsibility for lost items, and may offer you the option of adding insurance to your shipment if you want it.

Shipping insurance is often available via the United States Postal Service up to a certain dollar amount for every kind of shipping except for First Class Mail. Making sure your jewelry or watch item is insured before your seller ships it is extremely important—it not only protects you against an irresponsible or potentially fraudulent seller, it also guarantees you're reimbursed in case thieves snatch your package en route to your house. Jewelry theft through mail or courier is a major problem both in the United States and internationally.

Feedback: A Critical Social Custom

As you've already learned, feedback tells other eBayers everything they need to know about you as a responsible community member. Sellers live and die by their feedback, which is why this step of the buying process is so important.

Tit for Tat

Sellers will typically wait for you to make the first move when it comes to submitting feedback. That's because they need to protect themselves from buyers who dole out negative response. So it's up to you to make the first move. Wait until your item arrives. Inspect it to make sure everything looks acceptable, that the item is in good shape and appears to be as advertised. Once you're satisfied, you should provide positive feedback to the seller. To do so:

1. Log in, click My eBay, and click Won on the left menu.

2. On the line that lists the item you've just received, click Leave Feedback in the Action column.

3. Select the radio button next to Positive (see Figure 7.7).

4. Enter a brief comment about the transaction. You can either leave a generic comment ("A+++ SELLER! HIGHLY RECOMMEND!") or comments specific to the transaction ("Great communication! Loved the earrings!").

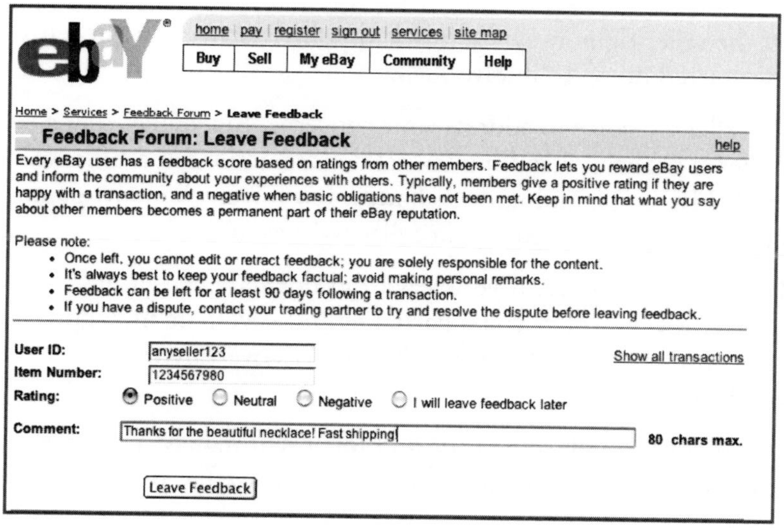

Figure 7.7

Leaving feedback for your seller is one of the most important parts of the buying process.

Is Honesty the Best Policy?

We're so used to providing our true opinion about everything—from service in a restaurant on a reply card left at the cash register to the quality of a novel in comments on a bookseller's Web site. On eBay, however, it's important to curb your honest feelings, except in extreme occasions. You need to reserve your neutral and negative feedback for occasions where the seller truly did not come through for you, despite your repeated attempts.

Here's why: Sellers dread negative feedback, anything that pulls down their feedback score. If you leave them neutral or negative feedback, they may get vindictive and retaliate by leaving *you* negative feedback. So if you're going to take that chance, it should be worth it.

If you've had a lukewarm experience with a seller—spotty communication, prolonged or inadequate shipping, or a problem with the condition or authenticity of the piece you receive—take the following steps before resorting to negative feedback:

1. Review the seller's terms to make sure the problem you've encountered hasn't been covered in the seller's contingencies. For example, if you haven't seen the item for a couple of weeks, make sure the seller hasn't claimed the right to wait 30 days before shipping in her written terms.

2. Contact the seller right away. Calmly and politely state your concerns and how you're hoping to resolve them.

3. Give the seller a chance to address your concerns. Remember that a PowerSeller is probably handling several dozen auctions at a time, so she is probably corresponding with quite a few buyers. So don't panic or react if you don't hear from your seller right away.

4. Be willing to compromise. If your seller did not state her refund policy in her terms, but offers you a partial refund if you are unhappy with your purchase, consider that to be a seller's overture to making good on the deal.

5. Remain patient through some back and forth. Ultimately, a seller is going to want to make you happy so she can salvage her positive feedback.

6. Only when you believe the seller has been blatantly irresponsible, fraudulent, or hostile without trying to work things out, and you feel the need to warn the eBay community about the seller, should you decide to leave negative feedback. But consider this long and hard before you make this decision, and be aware that the seller may very well leave you negative feedback in return.

chapter 8

The Good, the Bad, and the Ugly

You've heard the stories: the friend of a friend who sent $1,000 for an exercise machine or a stereo to a seller with a feedback score in the hundreds, only to have the seller vanish—e-mail account turned off, phone number disconnected—before the friend receives her goods. I won't deny it: These things happen. But the *stories* about these incidents are far more prevalent than the incidents themselves. Indeed, for the most part, any horror stories you hear about bad deals on eBay are urban legends, in the same category as the tale about the woman who had her finger cut off by frustrated ring thieves. In truth, according to eBay, only *0.01 percent* of all transactions result in reported cases of fraud. Put another way, only a few hundred out of the millions of transactions that occur on eBay each day go wrong. Of course, if you're one of the handful of buyers who gets duped, this is little consolation. If you suspect that you are among the unlucky few, don't panic; read on to decide what to do next.

How Bad Is Bad?

If you're a relatively new buyer on eBay, it's easy to jump to conclusions when things don't work out as expected. The first time I ever bought anything on eBay, I was so nervous that when my item hadn't arrived after a week, I immediately assumed I'd been ripped off. Of course, that was not the case; in the end, I received my items with no problems. But those few days of feeling the lump in my throat, of not sleeping at night because I was worried I'd fallen for the oldest trick in the book, were not happy ones.

A bad transaction comes in many shapes and sizes. Here are a few possible scenarios:

- Your seller suddenly disappears off the face of the earth, and you never receive your item even though you paid for it.

- Your seller claims to have shipped the item, but it never arrives.

- The item arrives, but it looks nothing like the picture in the seller's listing or like how the seller described it.

- The item you receive appears to be a counterfeit or to have fake stones or metal, despite having been advertised as "genuine."

Resolving the Problem on Your Own

The first thing you should do if you are dissatisfied with a transaction—if the item doesn't meet your expectations, or it hasn't arrived in what you consider a timely manner—is to re-read the auction's item description. You may well find some kind of stipulation that you missed or forgot about that explains the situation. Take the case of the delayed item that I previously described; when I re-read the listing description, I discovered that the seller's published shipping policy gave him *three weeks* to mail a sold item. That was a condition I had missed on my first read-through, and it explained the long delay in receiving my item. Although I was disappointed, I couldn't exactly argue with him, because it was my own fault that I hadn't read the shipping policy carefully.

If re-reading the item listing doesn't resolve the issue, your next step is to rule out the very real possibility that what is happening is really just the result of a big misunderstanding. That's why, before taking any other steps, it's imperative that you make a good-faith effort to get in touch with the seller to discuss your grievance. For example, if you're unsatisfied with the item, e-mail the seller to ask whether you can return it for a refund. Likewise, if an item never arrived, e-mail the seller to inform him of the situation, and work with him to track the package. (Of course, you should also call your post office or courier service to see whether they dropped the package at a neighbor's house or were otherwise unable to deliver the package.)

E-mail Etiquette

I am a stickler for service, so I'm the first one to get emotional when an eBay transaction doesn't go as smoothly as it should. Furthermore, I'm a wimp, and am therefore much more confident when I can tell people off via e-mail rather than face-to-face or over the phone. Unfortunately for me, these two qualities make for a dangerous combination; because of them, I am frequently tempted to use e-mail as a weapon, shooting off rude accusations to a seller whenever something doesn't go my way. I am here to tell you, however, that there's nothing more important in your dealings with eBay members than to remain polite and businesslike in all your e-mail communications, no matter how frustrated you become.

Why? Well, for one thing, your interaction with your eBay seller is a business transaction. If the seller is a professional (and you'll know from his feedback score whether he is), he will react in a businesslike way to your polite and reasonable request for retribution if an item isn't quite right, because he cares about building repeat business and a solid reputation. There's no need to fly off the handle or make accusations. In fact, if your e-mail is rude, irrational, or otherwise crazy-sounding, it's possible he'll dismiss you altogether, which means you won't get what you want.

Here's an example: A couple of years ago, I purchased an antique mantle clock as a gift for some friends who had just bought a century-old house with a beautiful fireplace. The photos accompanying the auction listing showed that the clock was slightly worn, but it had lots of character, and was described by the seller as being in working condition. When the clock arrived, however, it didn't work. I wound it and tinkered with it, but it would only run for a few minutes at a time before shuddering to a stop.

I was outraged. The seller had obviously sold me something that didn't work, and now I was stuck with this broken clock that I could not, in good taste, present to my friends! In my fury, I began to dash off an angry e-mail to the seller: "The clock arrived today and it doesn't work. It runs for a few minutes and then stops. You clearly misrepresented the condition of this piece, and I want my money back!" But then common sense prevailed. I set the unsent e-mail aside, and eventually, after I had cooled down, I revised my message. "The clock arrived and it is beautiful," I wrote. "But I can't seem to get it to run more than a few minutes at time. Your auction did say the clock was in working condition. Can you please help?"

Well, the seller wrote back right away, and he was *mortified*. It turned out he was a clockmaker who knew a lot about repairing timepieces, and he explained that sometimes the delicate inner workings of a clock can get thrown off slightly in the shipping process. He worked with me via e-mail, back and forth, to provide instructions on how to fix the clock myself, and when that didn't work, he recommended several reputable clock-repair professionals in my area. Through every communication, he was helpful and apologetic, which is certainly *not* the demeanor of a seller who had knowingly sold a broken clock! Had I started our dialog on a different note, I might not have secured his help in getting the clock to work again.

On eBay and in life, I have found that you get farther with people by killing them with kindness—being polite, nice, and relatively open-minded, while still remaining firm with your request. People react more reasonably when they are not on the defensive. I try to use the same tone and word choice that I employ when sending e-mails at work: professional, neutral, and unemotional. I try to start the e-mail on a positive note, then state the issue and ask how the seller can work with me to resolve the problem. This puts the ball in her court and launches a dialog that results in compromise rather than anger and hurt feelings.

Dealing with Missing Packages

If several days have passed since your seller said he shipped your item, but there's been no sign of the package on your doorstep, you're undoubtedly growing concerned. Before you assume the worst, however, take into consideration that the shipment could simply be delayed—for example, First Class Mail can sometimes, inexplicably, take several weeks.

If a more significant span of time has passed and you *still* haven't seen the package, contact the seller to keep him apprised of the situation. If he used a courier service that offers tracking, he'll be able to contact the service to find out the status of the delivery. If the package continues to remain MIA for longer than 21 days after the shipment date, the seller will need to file an insurance claim with the courier service (assuming you purchased insurance on the package) and reimburse your money. This might take several weeks to resolve, so be patient; and as long as the seller continues to communicate and work with you to resolve the situation, you should treat the incident as a missing package, not as a fraud case. If, on the other hand, the seller is incommunicative or resists your requests for reimbursement, it's possible that he never shipped your item at all. In that case, you should file a claim with eBay. See the section "Reporting the Case to eBay" later in this chapter for details.

Requesting the Seller's Phone Number

If your e-mails don't go through or the seller doesn't respond, or if you've been trading e-mails but simply can't resolve the issue, request the seller's phone number from eBay and call him to talk the issue through. To request a seller's phone number, do the following:

1. Click the Advanced Search link in the top-right corner of any screen on eBay.

2. Click Find Contact Information on the left navigation bar.

3. On the page shown in Figure 8.1, enter the seller's user ID, and then enter the item number of the transaction.

4. eBay will send you an e-mail message containing the seller's first and last name, address, and telephone number. The seller will also receive an e-mail with your contact information.

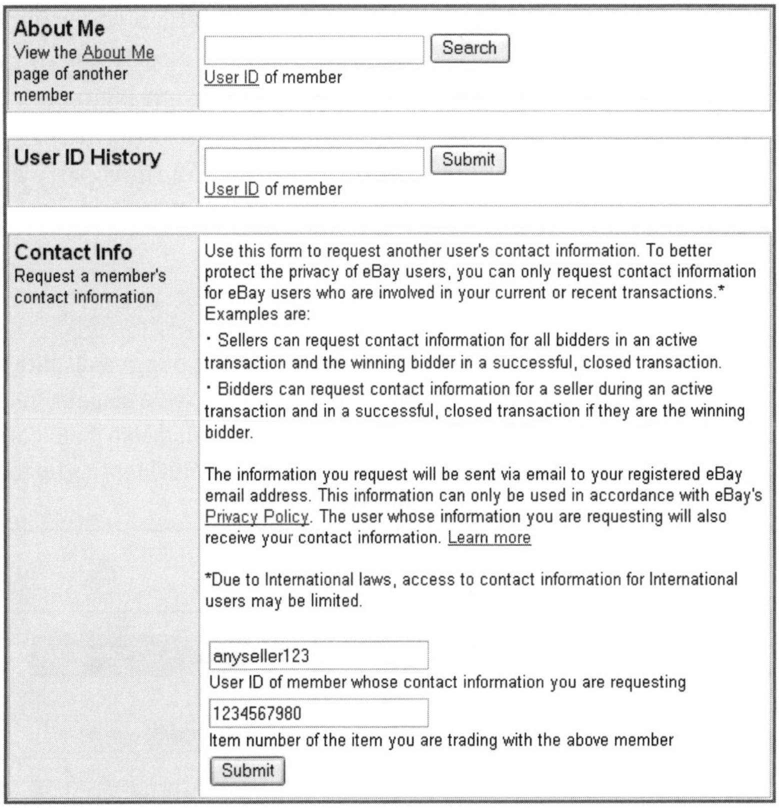

About Me
View the About Me
page of another
member

	Search

User ID of member

User ID History

	Submit

User ID of member

Contact Info
Request a member's
contact information

Use this form to request another user's contact information. To better protect the privacy of eBay users, you can only request contact information for eBay users who are involved in your current or recent transactions.* Examples are:

• Sellers can request contact information for all bidders in an active transaction and the winning bidder in a successful, closed transaction.

• Bidders can request contact information for a seller during an active transaction and in a successful, closed transaction if they are the winning bidder.

The information you request will be sent via email to your registered eBay email address. This information can only be used in accordance with eBay's Privacy Policy. The user whose information you are requesting will also receive your contact information. Learn more

*Due to International laws, access to contact information for International users may be limited.

anyseller123
User ID of member whose contact information you are requesting

1234567980
Item number of the item you are trading with the above member

Submit

Figure 8.1

In the event you need to call your seller about an issue, you can request your seller's contact information from eBay.

Your Next Move

You'll find that on eBay, most grievances can be resolved through simple communication. Although the process might not always be pleasant, in the end, both you and seller will be happier if the transaction ends satisfactorily. If playing peacemaker doesn't work, however, there are some formal steps you can take.

Mediation

You have been in communication with the seller, but the two of you simply cannot agree on a compromise to resolve the problem you're having. Fortunately, eBay works with SquareTrade (http://www.squaretrade.com), an online dispute-resolution service that will mediate your dispute and help you arrive at a fair agreement. Simply visit the SquareTrade site and file a case by entering your user ID and the eBay item number in question, as shown in Figure 8.2. SquareTrade will get in touch with the seller and invite him to participate in the mediated negotiation. Sometimes, the intervention of a third party is all it takes to reach an agreement.

Note

Be aware that, unlike in a court of law, SquareTrade will not take sides in a dispute. If asked, the service will provide a recommendation for how to resolve a dispute, but it will not declare one party the "winner" of the argument. The service also does not have the power to enforce any final ruling or recommendations it provides; it's up to both parties to follow through on the final agreement.

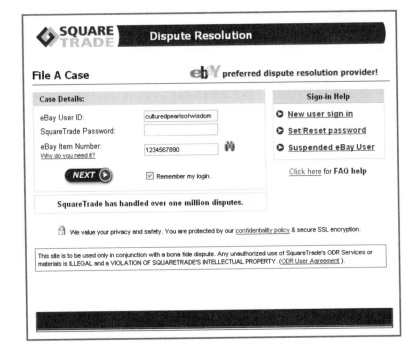

Figure 8.2

SquareTrade can help you initiate a mediated dispute-resolution case with your seller, so you can work things out before they get too ugly.

Reporting the Case to eBay

If you have had no luck getting through to the seller, or if you were sold an item fraudulently, you should report the case to eBay. Although eBay can't chase down fraudulent sellers on behalf of victimized buyers, the site does run the eBay Safe Harbor program to help investigate claims, and will suspend sellers if they are found to be committing fraud. So although reporting the incident won't do much to help you recoup your losses, doing so may, at the very least, help prevent the same thing that happened to you from happening to other buyers.

To report the case to eBay, do the following:

1. On eBay's home page, click Security Center on the bottom navigation bar.

2. Click the green Report a Problem button on the Security Center page.

3. In the top menu, select Report problems with other eBay members.

4. In the second menu, select Problems with sellers.

5. Select the statement that best represents your case in the third menu. Click Continue.

6. On the next page, click Email.

7. You'll be directed to an e-mail form that is specific to the problem you're reporting, as shown in Figure 8.3. Complete the requested information and click Send Email.

Using eBay's Buyer Protection Program

Reporting the case to eBay, as described in the preceding section, is your first step in resolving an issue. After you do, eBay will get back in touch with you to describe the next steps you should take, which usually involve providing more information so eBay can track down and stop the seller from hurting more buyers.

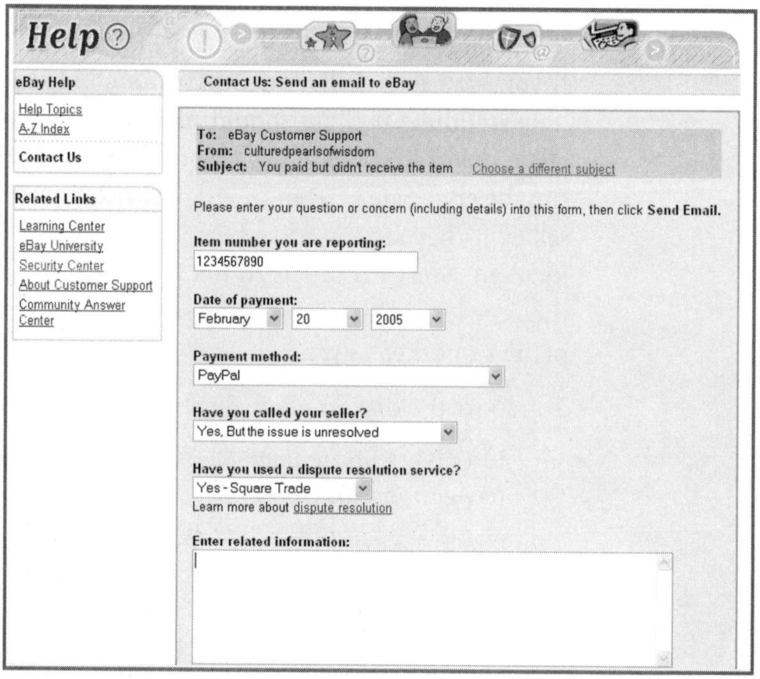

Figure 8.3

Your first step when you feel you've been defrauded is to report the case to eBay Customer Support.

But where does that leave you? If you've followed eBay protocol and reported the case, but you've been unable to get your money back after 30 days, you'll be pleased to learn that eBay offers a Buyer Protection Program that will reimburse you for your item up to $200 (the amount depends on the item's sale price), minus a $25 processing fee, provided you file a fraud alert first. You're eligible to file a fraud alert 30 days after the auction closing (after that milestone has passed, you have 30 more days to file the alert). Here's how it's done:

1. On eBay's home page, click Help in the top menu, and then click Transaction Problems. On the screen that appears, click Protection for Buyers, and then Fraud Protection.

2. Scroll down to the second table and click File a fraud alert now.

3. Click Submit a new complaint.

4. Under the question Do you feel another eBay member has defrauded you?, click Yes.

5. Carefully read the guidelines for submitting a claim to determine whether you are eligible to receive protection coverage. If you are indeed eligible, click Continue and enter the requested information about your transaction. As shown in Figure 8.4, you'll be asked for the item number and other details about the transaction.

Online Fraud Complaint Reporting Form

This is the contact information that eBay has on file for you. Is this information correct?

Stacey Gordon
Oakland, CA 94611
United States

Primary Phone: (510) 555-1212
Secondary Phone:
Fax:
EMail: jewelry@night-writer.com

[Click here if the above information is wrong]

If the above information is correct, were you the bidder in the transaction?

Item # was: 1234567890 and [I was bidder]

Remember, you must submit an Online Fraud Complaint within 60 days from the end of the listing and mail in a Fraud Protection Claim within 90 days of the end of the listing.

Figure 8.4

Use eBay's Online Fraud Complaint Reporting Form screen to submit a formal claim so you can seek reimbursement through eBay's Buyer Protection Program.

Note

Be aware that the Buyer Protection Program doesn't reimburse for everything. If an item was lost or damaged during shipping, or if you paid using a wire-transfer service such as Western Union, eBay can't reimburse you. Read the guidelines carefully before submitting a claim.

You will be duly informed via e-mail if eBay accepts your claim; the message will contain a link to a claim form, which you can download and print. Submit the form to eBay via fax or mail *within 90 days of the auction close date*, along with a proof of payment, a denial of reimbursement from your credit-card company (see the next section for more information on that), and a letter of authenticity based on an independent appraisal of your item (in the event you were required by eBay to prove that your item was misrepresented). A claims administrator will contact you within 45 days after you mail or fax your claim.

Other Ways to Get Your Money Back

If eBay's Buyer Protection Program doesn't reimburse you for all (or any of) the amount you lost, you might be able to get the remainder of your money back from the following sources:

■ **PayPal Buyer Protection.** If you used PayPal to pay for your purchase, you're covered for up to $1,000 for transactions gone wrong (see Figure 8.5). Your seller must have had the PayPal Buyer Protection icon displayed in his seller information box on the auction, and you must have used PayPal to pay for the item.

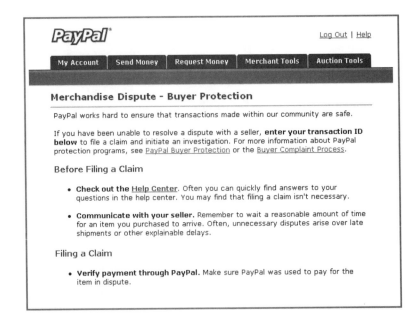

Figure 8.5

PayPal Buyer Protection is one way you might be able to get some of your money back if your deal goes bad.

■ **SquareTrade.** If you buy from a seller who is enrolled in the Square-Trade program, you could receive as much as $250 in reimbursement if the seller defrauds you.

■ **Credit card protection.** If you use a major credit card to pay for your transaction, you possibly have built-in protection. Most Visa, Master-Card, and American Express cards give at least partial refunds if you fall victim to consumer fraud.

Reporting the Case Elsewhere

If you feel the case of fraud is really serious—a seller blatantly stole money from you for a high-value item, or deliberately sold you a misrepresented item (such as a fake gemstone or a counterfeit)—you should report it to agencies not affiliated with eBay as well reporting it to eBay. After all, if the seller makes it a habit to defraud buyers, or is part of a ring of fraudulent sellers, you'll want to warn other buyers before the same thing happens to them. Also, you want to make sure the seller is stopped, for good, and punished if possible. Some of your options include

■ **Internet Fraud Complaint Center (http://www1.ifccfbi.gov).** The FBI and the National White Collar Crime Center work together through the Internet Fraud Complaint Center to investigate large-scale or repeat cases of fraud. At this Web site, shown in Figure 8.6, you can fill out a simple form, and the center will alert the proper authorities to begin an investigation of a civil or criminal complaint.

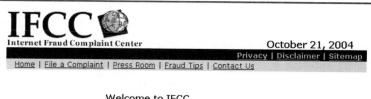

IFCC
Internet Fraud Complaint Center

October 21, 2004

Privacy | Disclaimer | Sitemap

Home | File a Complaint | Press Room | Fraud Tips | Contact Us

**Report Terrorist
Activity** (click here)

Filing a Complaint
How to file
Information Requested

Statistics

Partners

IFCC Warnings NEW

Welcome to IFCC

The Internet Fraud Complaint Center (IFCC) is a partnership between the Federal Bureau of Investigation (FBI) and the National White Collar Crime Center (NW3C).

IFCC's mission is to address fraud committed over the Internet. For victims of Internet fraud, IFCC provides a convenient and easy-to-use reporting mechanism that alerts authorities of a suspected criminal or civil violation. For law enforcement and regulatory agencies at all levels, IFCC offers a central repository for complaints related to Internet fraud, works to quantify fraud patterns, and provides timely statistical data of current fraud trends.

File a Complaint

This program is brought to you by the Federal Bureau of Investigation and the National White Collar Crime Center

NW3C
NATIONAL WHITE COLLAR CRIME CENTER

top | home | about us | press room | file a complaint | statistics | contact us
privacy | disclaimer | site map

Figure 8.6

The Internet Fraud Complaint Center will pass your claim on to the proper authorities.

- **Federal Trade Commission (http://www.ftc.gov).** The FTC doesn't investigate individual complaints, but it does enter e-commerce complaints into a national database accessible by law-enforcement agencies, and it can use your information to pursue criminal action against fraudulent sellers. The FTC takes a particular interest in misrepresentation of jewelry and gemstones, so if a seller has misled you, you should definitely take the case to the FTC.

- **National Fraud Information Center (http://www.fraud.org).** Run by the National Consumers League, this center provides a form for reporting consumer fraud cases, and promises to pass along the information to the appropriate law-enforcement agency. The site also features articles and resources for investigating sources and signs of fraud.

Danger from the Outside: Phishing

Although there are a few dishonest sellers out there, these days, you're probably less safe when you're *off* the eBay site than when you're on it. Why? Because clever crooks have discovered the art of *phishing*, which is a slang term for using deceptive e-mails to fool you into giving credit-card or other private information. These e-mails appear to come from eBay (see Figure 8.7), and typically warn you of a compromised account or possible account deactivation if you don't update your information. Then they include a link that appears to point to an eBay page. If you click on the link, you're whisked to a site that looks exactly like eBay—but it isn't. And once you've entered your information, these identity thieves can use it to their advantage before you even realize what happened.

It's not just credit-card information these crooks are seeking. Some will try to fool you into sharing your user ID and password, then hijack your account information so they can list fraudulent auctions under your name.

The way to avoid becoming the victim of phishing is to be skeptical of *any* e-mail communications with links that appear to point to eBay, especially those that request private account information. Only enter information such as credit-card numbers if you have *typed* in eBay's Web site address yourself, not if you've clicked a link in an e-mail to get to the site (there have

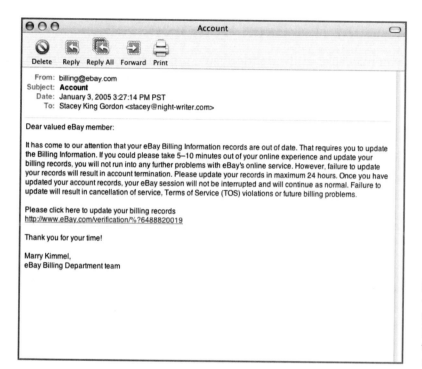

○ ○ ○   Account

Delete   Reply Reply All Forward Print

From: billing@ebay.com
Subject: **Account**
Date: January 3, 2005 3:27:14 PM PST
To: Stacey King Gordon <stacey@night-writer.com>

Dear valued eBay member:

It has come to our attention that your eBay Billing Information records are out of date. That requires you to update the Billing Information. If you could please take 5–10 minutes out of your online experience and update your billing records, you will not run into any further problems with eBay's online service. However, failure to update your records will result in account termination. Please update your records in maximum 24 hours. Once you have updated your account records, your eBay session will not be interrupted and will continue as normal. Failure to update will result in cancellation of service, Terms of Service (TOS) violations or future billing problems.

Please click here to update your billing records
http://www.eBay.com/verification/%?6488820019

Thank you for your time!

Marry Kimmel,
eBay Billing Department team

Figure 8.7

This e-mail looks like it's from eBay, but it really isn't. If you click this link, it will take you to a site that isn't on eBay's servers.

been reported cases of phishers using code to make the site appear to have an eBay URL, even when it doesn't). Also, always be sure that before you enter any secure information, the address bar indicates you are in secure mode (it will say https:// instead of http://).

Note

eBay is only one of the sites used by phishers as a front to steal account information. More often, you'll see e-mails that appear to come from credit-card companies or your bank, asking you to log in and verify your account information, password, and other protected data. Don't fall for it! These services would never ask you to do such a thing. If you have a question about whether such a request is legitimate, call your financial institution's customer service number (the one on your monthly statement or the back of your card, *not* the one included in the e-mail you received) and ask a live representative if account verification is indeed needed. You can then take care of any necessary updates over the phone.

If Your Account Has Been Compromised…

If you think you may have inadvertently shared private information with an illegitimate party, you need to move swiftly. Immediately do the following:

1. Log in to eBay and change your password right away.

2. File a fraud report with eBay.

3. Contact your bank and credit-card company, and ask them to notify you of any suspicious activity. If necessary, cancel your accounts and open new ones. Watch your statements carefully for unauthorized charges or withdrawals.

4. Report identity theft to the three credit bureaus: Equifax, Transunion, and Experian.

Just as you would if you found out somebody stole your wallet or your mail, you'll want to prevent this unfortunate incident from haunting you forever. Be as vigilant and proactive as possible, and don't leave anything to chance.

part 3

eBay for Sellers

chapter 9

From Buyer to Seller

Beginning your life on eBay as a buyer gives you a chance to familiarize yourself with the site, learn your way around, start to understand a little about how the natives behave, and get a feel for how vast the eBay jewelry and watch universe is. After your first several purchases, you'll probably start to feel like you're an eBay expert.

But while you're having so much fun on your eBay shopping spree, the entrepreneurial part of your brain is no doubt starting to find its voice. "I could do this too," you begin to tell yourself. "I understand enough about jewelry to make a living on eBay."

That very well might be true. Lots of people in the world now sell on eBay full-time, and many more supplement their steady incomes with solid eBay sales. But before you start indulging your fantasies of quitting your day job, holing yourself up in your spare bedroom, and making millions off your grandmother's (and other people's grandmothers') jewels, there are some important things to understand about selling on eBay. Namely:

- **You have to know your stuff.** Especially with fine jewelry and vintage costume jewelry, you can't just slap an item up for auction without being fully educated about what it is and what it's worth. You could get in quite a bit of trouble—as a worst-case scenario, being suspended from eBay or even facing legal action—by doing so.

- **Jewelry is a tricky business.** It can get messy. You have so many issues with which you must contend: gemstone treatments, fake gems, counterfeits. If you're not a professional, you'll need to start slowly and keep learning along the way.

- **Timing is everything.** A combination of strategy and luck will determine whether your item sells at a good price or doesn't sell at all. It takes awhile to figure out what will work for you.

- **And speaking of time...** Selling on eBay requires a substantial time investment. Managing, communicating, packing, shipping, and handling returns can eat up hours in your day. Your fun and lucrative hobby may well take over your life.

And Now the Good News

And yet there are millions of people who sell on eBay worldwide, thousands of them specializing in jewelry and watches. Why? Quite simply, because it's an easy way to make a profit. Your consumer base is made up of thousands of people, with a range of tastes, personalities, situations, and expendable incomes. You've got men shopping for the perfect engagement ring or anniversary present; shoppers always on the lookout for pieces that let them express themselves; collectors who will jump all over anything that's Art Deco or Bakelite; or just bored browsers looking for entertainment or inspiration. And depending on what you're selling, any of these consumers could get emotionally attached to your item and bid up the price so that you're making back your investment many times over.

You've heard the adage "one person's junk is another person's treasure." It's the classic philosophy of the yard sale and the flea market. And it can be adapted perfectly to the eBay sellers' model, even if what you're selling isn't really junk. Even if you pay a small price for an item, you have the potential to resell it at a gargantuan profit if buyers take a shine to it. As long as you're fairly representing what you're selling, it's perfectly within your rights to sell an item that you purchased for $15 and collect a price of $200. The brilliant thing about eBay is that your selling price equals *the item's worth to somebody else*—and you have no way of predicting what that price will be.

Rules for Sellers

We already covered directions for setting up a seller's account in Chapter 1, "Getting Started on eBay," along with the basics of your user's agreement.

To ensure that sellers engage in fair trading practices, however, there are a number of rules that are specific to sellers (see Figure 9.1). You should make sure that you understand them before listing your first auction. Visit http://pages.ebay.com/policies/ia/rules_for_sellers.html to read all the rules.

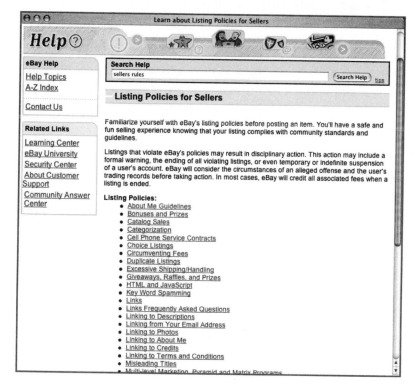

Figure 9.1

eBay's rules for sellers are thorough, so you should review the Policies section in depth before you begin selling.

Here are a few highlights:

- **Sales outside of eBay.** You can't offer your buyers the opportunity to purchase your item outside of eBay. Most importantly, that means that you can't link to another site, such as your own e-commerce store on a different server than eBay's, to point potential buyers toward your other items for sale.

- **"Shill" bidding.** This is a huge faux pas in the eBay world. *Shilling* is when you or someone you know places fake bids to raise the selling price of the item. If eBay catches you at this, they could suspend your account. eBay even recommends that you refrain from allowing friends and family members to bid on your items to prevent the appearance of shilling.

- **Misleading titles.** You can't confuse buyers by comparing your item to something it's not. "Diamond and platinum bracelet," used as a description for a cubic zirconia and platinum rhodium-plated bracelet, is an example of a misleading title. "'Tiffany' necklace" if the necklace is not truly Tiffany is another. See more about this in Chapter 11, "Creating Compelling—and Legally Correct—Product Descriptions."

The most important rule to remember is that, as a seller, you are obligated to accept payment and ship the item when your buyer pays for it. You cannot list the item, sell it, and then change your mind. I'll cover more of these rules throughout this chapter.

Sourcing Your Goods

If you're considering selling jewelry or watches on eBay, the first question that probably comes to mind is: *How do I find items to sell?* After you've cleaned out your great-aunt's old costume jewelry and other pieces you no longer want from your dresser drawers, where do you go from there? Sourcing, or finding items to buy and resell, is a constant challenge for eBay sellers, and it often determines the difference between a successful and unsuccessful seller.

Sellers who have been using eBay for awhile will tell you that they have their own tricks and secrets that work reliably for them. Here are a few options you might consider:

- **Wholesale.** Buying wholesale enables you to purchase items in bulk at special prices. To do so legally, however, you're required to have a business license from your state, which recognizes you as a retail business, as well as a tax resale number. If you are a home-based business, your tax resale number (often called your tax ID number) is typically your Social Security number with a couple of letters tacked on to the end, but you do need to officially register it. A wholesaler will also require you to show a resale certificate that states you plan to resell whatever goods you're purchasing from him. To learn more about your state's requirements for a retail business license, state tax ID, and resale certificate, visit your state's Department of Revenue or Department of Taxation Web site (see Figure 9.2).

Figure 9.2

Your state's Department of Revenue—or in the case of my home state of California, the Franchise Tax Board—can provide you with information about obtaining a business license and a tax resale number so you can buy jewelry wholesale.

■ **Estate sales and auctions.** Especially for antique and vintage jewelry, estate sales can be clearinghouses of unique, valuable jewelry selling for deeply discounted prices. Your investment is weekend after weekend of showing up early at sales, and you'll probably see a lot more junk than you will valuables. Still, because estate sales are means for families or executors to profit by selling off property en masse, you'll often find very undervalued pieces at these events.

■ **Yard and rummage sales.** Although it might seem unlikely that you could find anything valuable at these sales alongside old kitchenware and ugly framed posters, it's sometimes unbelievable what people will get rid of when they're desperate to downsize. Yard sales can be good places to find good vintage jewelry, for example, because people sometimes sell it not realizing what it's worth.

■ **Buying from private sellers.** You can use community bulletin boards, newspaper classified ads, or online forums to announce that you purchase used jewelry. These ads could plant an idea in the head of a seller who is trying to find ways to make some extra cash and, at the same time, never knew what to do with the pearl necklace her grandmother left her.

■ **Other eBay auctions.** If you have a good eye, you might be able to buy jewelry at a deal and turn it quickly at a higher price. Many sellers do this regularly.

■ **Retail stores.** Every once in awhile, you can find super discounts at the costume jewelry counter of a department store or in a boutique gift or clothing store. The retailers, in an attempt to clean out the stockroom and make room for more fashionable goods, could mark down nice fashion jewelry to a dollar or two. If you can find these deals, you might be able to profit nicely with the items on eBay.

■ **Thrift stores.** Steer clear of the "thrift stores" that are actually funky boutiques positioned as secondhand stores (ever since thrift became trendy, a lot of these kinds of stores sell "thrift" goods at prices that exceed even retail). Instead, head to the real thrift stores: Goodwill, Salvation Army, American Cancer Society stores, and other shops that benefit charities. Occasionally you'll find treasures that are priced surprisingly low.

■ **Your own jewelry creations.** If you have an artistic streak, or if you have a hobby of designing and creating bead jewelry, eBay may be a great place to market your wares. Buyers love unique pieces that have been handcrafted, such as the necklace pictured in Figure 9.3. Over time, you might even move into using more expensive stones, such as cultured pearls or semiprecious colored gemstones.

Figure 9.3

If you're passionate about jewelry design, eBay provides a way to profit from your hobby, or even build a following for a budding career. Necklace designed by Samantha Cooper of Scoop Design, Oakland, Calif.

Profit Talk

To the inexperienced seller, buying jewelry at rock-bottom prices and reselling it for potentially 10 or 20 times more than you paid might seem thorny, even dishonest. But eBay is the ultimate capitalist marketplace, and that demand drives the price. As long as you are being completely forthright in your product description and disclosures, there's absolutely nothing wrong with making a healthy profit. In fact, it's the whole point.

eBay experts have put together complex formulas to weigh the amount of time you'll spend and fees you'll pay to sell goods using the online marketplace, compared to the amount of profit you'll need to earn to make it all worth your time. In fact, one expert claims that, if you're selling on eBay all or most of your time, you must make around $20 on every sale, or you're wasting valuable Internet bandwidth (not to mention spending way too much time hunched over your computer screen). Your primary goal as a seller is to find dependable ways to buy low and sell high.

Of course, selling on eBay takes a lot of trial and error, and when you're just starting out, making a huge profit may not be as important as building feedback and getting a feel for what buyers like and how they behave. So there's no need to be aggressive just yet. Get your feet wet and take it slow so you can get into a good groove.

Sellers' Fees

Sellers are the source of eBay's income. For the privilege of access to thousands of buyers, an easy-to-use infrastructure, and advertising that draws traffic to the site, sellers are required to pay nominal fees.

The first fee a seller faces is to place the item listing in the first place. As Table 9.1 shows, you will pay more money the higher the starting price of the item is.

Table 9.1 Listing Fees*

Starting or Reserve Price	Insertion Fee
$0.01–$0.99	$0.30
$1.00–$9.99	$0.35
$10.00–$24.99	$0.60
$25.00–$49.99	$1.20
$50.00–$199.99	$2.40
$200.00–$499.99	$3.60
$500.00 or more	$4.80

Note that these fees are as of this writing, and are subject to change at eBay's discretion.

After the item sells, eBay collects another fee—a commission or finder's fee, if you will. As you see in Table 9.2, you pay a percentage of the final sales price on a sliding scale that depends on the price range of the item.

Table 9.2 Final Fees*

Closing Price	Fee (% of Final Sales Price)
Item not sold	No fee
$0.01–$25.00	5.25%
$25.01–$1,000.00	5.25% of the initial $25.00, plus 2.75% of the balance of the final sales price
$1,000.01 or more	5.25% of the initial $25.00, plus 2.75% of the initial $25.00–$1,000.00, plus 1.50% of the remaining closing value balance

Note that these fees are as of this writing, and are subject to change at eBay's discretion.

Before you scramble to get out your calculator, note that eBay makes tracking and paying these fees relatively easy. You can regularly check your account status using My eBay, and use PayPal to pay the fees as they add up. Or, you can set up your preferences to pay your account automatically every month. You'll learn how to pay your fees later in this chapter.

In addition to charging fees when you post and sell an item, eBay charges for use of a number of add-ons and tools to give sellers a leg up. For example, you'll pay an extra fee for things like special placement in search engine results, reserve prices, and auction management software. I'll discuss these options later in this section, but be aware that your fees could be higher if you choose to use them.

Posting an Auction

Posting an auction is easy. Once you're logged in, simply do the following:

1. Log in to eBay and click the Sell tab.

2. Click the Sell Your Item button, shown in Figure 9.4.

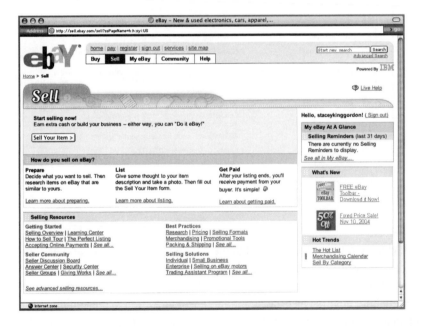

Figure 9.4

To start selling, simply click the Sell Your Item button, and you're on your way.

3. Click the Sell your item at online auction option button and click Continue.

4. Under Main Category, click the Jewelry & Watches option button, as shown in Figure 9.5. Then click Continue.

5. Select a subcategory from the upper-left box. When you've made your selection, the next level of category list will automatically appear in the upper-right box. Continue selecting subcategories until there are no more sublevels to choose from.

	Sell Your Item step 1 of 5: Category	
○	Consumer Electronics	Home Theater, MP3 Players, TVs
○	Crafts	Craft supplies of all kinds: Needlearts, Scrapbooking, Painting, Ceramics, Woodworking and more!
○	Dolls & Bears	Barbies, figures, miniature houses & Cherished Teddies
○	DVDs & Movies	DVDs, VHS tapes, laserdiscs, film, and other movie formats
○	Entertainment Memorabilia	Movie, television, & music memorabilia including posters, props, photos, & rock-n-roll items
○	Gift Certificates	Gift Certificates for Restaurants, Department Stores, Clothing & Groceries
○	Health & Beauty	Beauty products such as perfume, makeup, face and body care and Health related items - massage, weight management; medical supplies.
○	Home & Garden	Furniture, Kitchen, Home Decor, Bed & Bath, Appliances, Tools, Lawn & Garden, Baby, Pets, & more…
◉	Jewelry & Watches	Fine, vintage and designer jewelry, watches, & jewelry supplies
○	Music	CDs, records, and other music formats
○	Musical Instruments	Guitars, woodwinds, percussion & pro audio equipment
○	Pottery & Glass	China, glass, pottery, porcelain & stoneware
○	Real Estate	Residential, commercial, timeshares & land
○	Sporting Goods	Sports Equipment, Apparel & Footwear, Golf, Cycling, Hunting, Fishing Fitness & More!
○	Sports Mem, Cards & Fan Shop	Current and Vintage Cards, Game Used, Autographed & Unsigned Sports Memorabilia, Licensed Team Apparel, and Sports Souvenirs.
○	Stamps	Scripophily, US & world stamps
○	Tickets	Concerts, sports events, theater & one-of-a-kind experiences
○	Toys & Hobbies	Action figures, bean bag plush, crafts & trains
○	Travel	Flights, cruises, hotels & luggage
○	Video Games	Games, game systems, internet game items, accessories & more

Figure 9.5

You're required to select one main category—in your case, Jewelry & Watches—in which you want to list your item.

Note

At this point, you have the option of selecting a second main category and accompanying subcategories in which you'd like to place the exact same listing. This doubles your chances of having your listing spotted and attracting bidders, since you can never anticipate how buyers will browse for an item. If you choose this option, you'll be charged double the item listing fee, but your final value fee (if the item sells) will be the same.

6. Enter the title of your auction. You're limited to 55 characters, so choose your words strategically, putting yourself in the mindset of the buyer to imagine which terms they might use to search for jewelry. If you have important information that doesn't fit in the title, you can add a subtitle for an additional fee.

7. Scroll down and enter your item description in the space shown in Figure 9.6. You have unlimited space here. See Chapter 11 for suggestions on how to write descriptions that work. When you're finished writing your description, click Continue.

Tip

Because the field for entering your information is so small, you might want to compose your description in a word-processing program such as Microsoft Word or a text editor such as Notepad, and then copy and paste it into eBay's form.

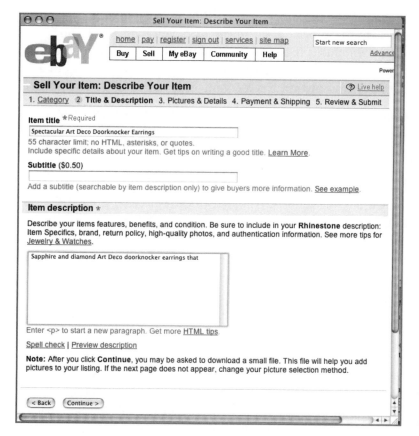

Figure 9.6

Craft your description in a word processor and then paste it into the form. As you write your title and description, keep in mind how buyers will most likely search for items.

8. Enter a starting price. Remember that the lower the price you enter, the more interest you'll likely generate from potential buyers. You also want to be sure, however, that you at least make your money back on the piece, and possibly make a profit. There are a few things you can do to determine a starting price:

   ■ Research the prices for which similar items have sold in the past. (See Chapter 2, "Doing Your Homework," for more information on researching sale prices by searching closed auctions.) If you're selling an item that tends to consistently command a high or at least fair sale price, then you're probably safe to start the price low to attract bidders.

   ■ Subtract a small percentage—say, 10 or 20 percent—from your item's acquisition price (that is, the price you paid when you bought the item). That way, you're still starting low enough to spark some interest in your auction, but not risking too big of a loss if the item only attracts a couple bidders.

   ■ If your piece is truly wonderful quality, or is particularly rare, unique, or a collector's item, you might want to consider starting higher than you ordinarily would. Why? Because shoppers will still find you if your item is adequately in-demand. A very low price will suggest to these wary hunters that your item is cheap, or that it's not what you say it is. A higher price (especially if it's still a good amount below what they'd find in a retail store) will help them feel safer. It might take a few different times listing your item to sell it, but you could be surprised at how much you end up earning.

9. If you like, enter a Buy It Now price, which is the "retail" price that a buyer can pay you to purchase the item before the first bid comes in. Buy It Now is an attractive option for sellers who know their item will be highly coveted by buyers. If a potential buyer opts to place a bid instead of paying the Buy It Now price, the Buy It Now option disappears—because, as a seller, you're obligated to entertain bids and sell your piece to the highest bidder. There's no extra charge to use Buy It Now, though you must meet certain criteria.

Note

To include a Buy It Now option in your auction, you must either have a feedback score of 10 or higher (if you don't have a PayPal account), have a feedback score of 5 or higher (if you have PayPal and accept it for payment), or use the eBay ID Verify service (in which you must allow a third-party service to conduct a background check to confirm your contact information and business status).

10. You also have the option to set a reserve price. Reserves on eBay are similar to those used in real-life auctions—they're secret price thresholds below which a seller will not sell the item. Bidders compete against each other to place the highest bid, but they also compete against the reserve, driving the price higher so the item will sell. Reserves are typically used for very high-priced items. eBay charges fees to use reserve prices, but will refund the fees if the item sells. See Table 9.3 for current fee listings.

Table 9.3 Reserve Fees*

Reserve Amount	Fee
Below $50	$1
$50-$199.99	$2
$200 or more	1% of reserve price (up to $100)

Note that these fees are as of this writing, and are subject to change at eBay's discretion.

Note

Sellers who want to move high-priced items without taking a loss like to use reserve prices so they can protect their profits without scaring off potential buyers. The problem is, because reserve prices are hidden from buyers, there are two hurdles for buyers to overcome: They not only have to outbid their fellow buyers, but they also need to attain some secret goal. A number of independent studies on the use of reserve prices in online auctions show that, on average, reserve auctions tend to result in fewer successful sales because buyers might be discouraged from bidding, or might stop bidding early because they don't know how close they are to the reserve. That said, if you must make a profit on an expensive item, that might be a chance you'll want to take.

11. Select the time limit for your auction from the Duration pull-down menu. The longer an item is on the site, the more chance you have for people to notice it. On the other hand, you might inspire bids faster and earlier if your auction ends sooner, because buyers don't like to bid too early and risk driving the price up. Weigh your options and choose one of the intervals: one, three, five, seven, or ten days (there is a small fee associated with the ten-day auction). Then select whether you want to start your auction right away or at a specified time.

12. Mark the Private Auction check box if you want to keep user IDs from being visible to bidders. Some sellers say they like to do this to protect their bidders in cases of highly competitive bidding, because there have been cases on eBay of user ID "stalking," where one buyer watches another user's bidding patterns expressly so she can swoop in and snipe that buyer's item. However, buyers are also somewhat suspicious of private auctions, so selecting this option can work against you. There is no extra fee for making an auction private.

13. Scroll down to the Add Pictures section, shown in Figure 9.7. You are eligible to upload one digital image free of charge with your listing. Additional pictures are available for a small fee. To add an image, click the Choose File button under Picture 1 and browse your hard drive for your image. When you find the file, select it, and then click Choose. For extra fees, you can also select one of eBay's upgrade options, including super-sized pictures and slide shows. For more information about how to create images for your site, see Chapter 11.

Tip

You also have the option of hosting images yourself using your own Web server space or a photo-hosting service such as Ofoto. To do this, upload your photo file to the site and copy the URL that points to the image. Then click Your Own Web Hosting under Add Pictures, and paste the URL in the Picture Web address field. Using the self-hosting option, you can also add a "slide show" of multiple images for a small fee (compared to the per-picture fee eBay charges for uploading images to its server); buyers will be able to scroll through a slide show of your images at the top of the auction listing. To activate this option, mark the Picture Show check box and add up to five URLs.

Figure 9.7

Choose a file from your hard drive and upload it to add a picture to your listing. Your first picture is free. Additional pictures, as well as enhancements to make your photos more attractive, are available at additional fees.

14. The Listing Designer allows you to add a background or border, and to arrange the layout of your auction list, for a small fee. This helps set your auction apart from the usual white and black descriptions. You can choose jewelry-specific themes or other backgrounds, like the one shown in Figure 9.8. The layout template allows you to decide how your text and images are placed on your page.

15. eBay gives you a number of tempting offers to help your listing get more traffic—for a fee. Most sellers choose the Gallery option, which adds your photo to your search engine listing. For sellers with more on the line, eBay offers the option to have the item listed in the Featured section (for $19.95) or to add boldface ($3) or color highlights ($5) to listings. These options are probably worth it only if you stand to make a healthy profit on your item. (Note that these fees were current as of this writing, and are subject to change.)

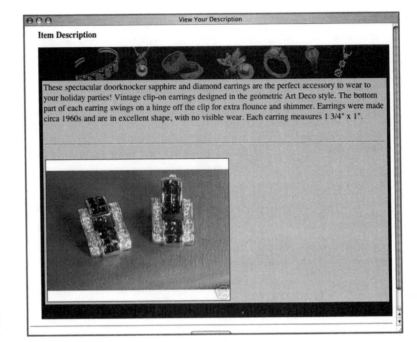

Figure 9.8

For a small fee, you can add a pre-designed background to make your auction listing more attractive.

Promoting Your Auctions Using eBay Upgrades

For serious sellers looking for ways to gain a competitive edge, eBay offers a number of upgrades and options that help sellers attract more attention for their auctions. Using these tools costs money, of course, but many sellers believe they're worth it. Here's a look at what's available for your auction success (note that the prices listed here are correct as of this writing, but are subject to change):

- **Gallery.** As mentioned, for 25 cents, you can have your photo added to the listing that buyers will see as they search and browse categories. A study conducted by eBay in 2003 showed that opting for the Gallery feature increased sellers' final sales price by an average of 11 percent. Figure 9.9 shows listings that use Gallery photos.

- **Bold.** This feature adds boldface formatting to your category auction listing, so it stands out from the rest of the auctions. The upgrade costs $1.

- **Highlight.** For $5, you can add a background color to your category auction listing to distinguish it further, as shown in Figure 9.10.

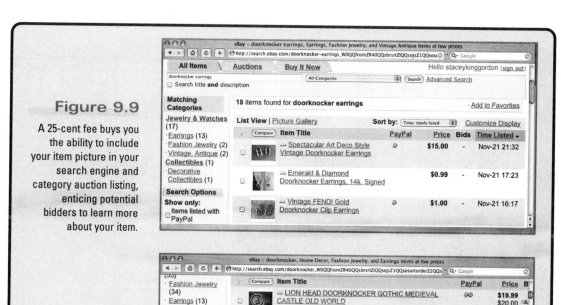

Figure 9.9

A 25-cent fee buys you the ability to include your item picture in your search engine and category auction listing, enticing potential bidders to learn more about your item.

Figure 9.10

The Highlight option adds background color to your auction listing.

- ■ **Border.** Add a frame around your auction listing for $3.

- ■ **Featured Plus.** On search results and category listings pages, eBay places a prominent box of featured listings to capture browsers' attention. You can have your auction added to this box for $19.95.

- ■ **Home Page Featured.** The ultimate upgrade, this feature rotates your auction listing with other paid listings in the Featured Items box on the eBay home page, as shown in Figure 9.11. The cost is $39.95, but for sellers who want to drive up the price of their item, it's prime placement for getting noticed, because eBay's home page attracts millions of page views a day. The only negative is that eBay cannot guarantee the listing will ever actually make it up. You have a pretty good chance that it will make it through the rotation, but it's not a sure thing.

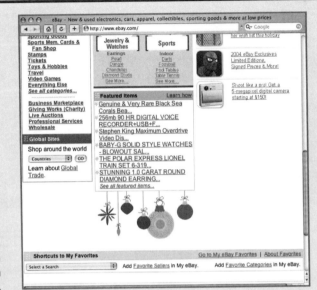

Figure 9.11

The fee is steep, but you can't beat the exposure when you opt to have your item featured on the eBay home page.

■ **Gift icon.** To inspire buyers who are shopping for that special someone, you can add a gift icon to your auction, as shown in Figure 9.12. This suggests to your buyer that your item would make a perfect gift. You can also specify any extra services you might offer, such as gift wrap or shipping directly to the gift recipient.

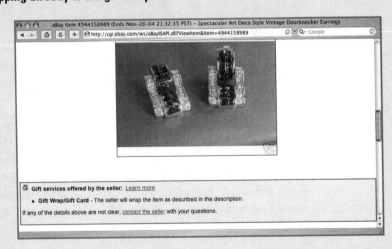

Figure 9.12

Adding a gift icon and a list of your gift services can inspire buyers who are shopping for special occasions.

16. If you're curious about how much traffic you've generated from a listing, you can opt to include a free page counter on your listing, which will track the number of hits you receive. Unless you have a specific reason for not wanting buyers to see your hits (for example, some sellers don't want the world to know if their auctions aren't generating impressive traffic), the visible counters are more convenient, because you have to log in to Andale, a separate site, to see the invisible results. After you've selected your counter, click Continue.

17. In the screen shown in Figure 9.13, select the check boxes next to the types of payment you wish to accept: PayPal, cashier's check or money order, personal check, or credit cards (if you have a merchant's account).

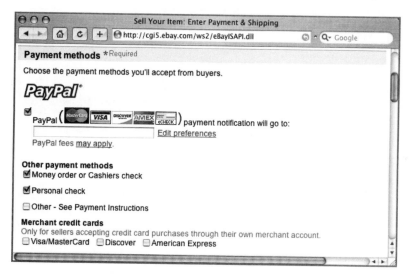

Figure 9.13

Select the check boxes next to the types of payments you are willing to accept from your buyers. Think carefully about what you have the time and patience to deal with—waiting for personal checks to clear and paying bank fees if they don't, for example.

18. Specify where you are willing to ship the item. You can click the Worldwide check box, or select specific areas of the world where you will ship the item.

19. Determine how you wish to charge for shipping. Your options are to charge buyers a flat rate or to calculate a rate based on the buyer's address. The advantage of choosing the Flat option is that buyers will see upfront what you plan to charge. To use that option, click the Flat tab, select the type of service you plan to use (see more about shipping services in Chapter 13, "Shipping Jewelry"), and then manually enter your shipping rate, as shown in Figure 9.14. Alternatively, click the Calculated tab, select your package weight and type, the

services you'll use for domestic and international shipping, your preference for insurance, and your own ZIP code. eBay will do the rest, calculating the shipping once the item has sold. Buyers won't be able see shipping costs before the item sells, although you can provide estimates in your item description if you wish.

Tip

To determine a flat fair price, click Research rates and services to open a pop-up window that will help you calculate rates.

Figure 9.14

You have the option of either determining a flat rate for your shipping, or allowing eBay to automatically calculate the shipping when the auction ends.

20. If you choose to accept returns, check the box beside Returns Accepted (leave it blank if you won't accept returns). Select from the pull-down menu the number of days within which a buyer must return an item to you: three, seven, fourteen, or thirty. Next, select Exchange, Merchandise Credit, or Money Back to establish how you will deal with returns. You can then enter up to 500 characters detailing your policies and conditions regarding returns.

Tip

Before you make your first sale, you'll want to anticipate anything that might go wrong with it in order to establish a comprehensive sales policy that spells out your expectations to sellers in no uncertain terms. See more about establishing your seller's policies in Chapter 12, "Sealing the Deal."

21. Use the Payment Instructions field to outline your specific terms on customer payments. Here is where you can set your own rules to protect yourself. For example, some sellers state that they will repost an item if they haven't received a communication or payment within so many days.

22. Click Continue. Now you can preview your listing. Proofread everything carefully for accuracy, and then click Submit Listing.

As long as you don't have any bids on your item, you can edit your listing after you post it. Just log in to My eBay, click Selling and then the name of your auction, and click Revise item to made edits. Learn more about editing your listing on in Chapter 12.

Paying Your eBay Fees

You can opt to pay any fees assessed by eBay manually or automatically. To pay your fees manually, do the following:

1. Log in to your eBay account and click My eBay.

2. On the left menu, under Selling, click My Account (see Figure 9.15).

3. Scroll down to My Seller Account Summary. You will see your current balance and a form that you can use to quickly pay off the balance. If you have a PayPal account, you can fill in the amount you want to pay and click Pay. You'll then be asked to log in to your PayPal account and can pay as you normally would. If you do not have a PayPal account, select one of the forms of payment underneath your payment to arrange to pay your balance.

Although paying your fees manually does the trick, you may prefer to pay them automatically. The benefits of setting up automatic payments is that you can be sure to pay your fees on time every month—and avoid the 1.5% late fee that eBay charges if you don't make your payments on time. Here's how to set up automatic payments:

1. Under Selling, click My Account.

2. Scroll down to the eBay Seller Fees header, and click Another method.

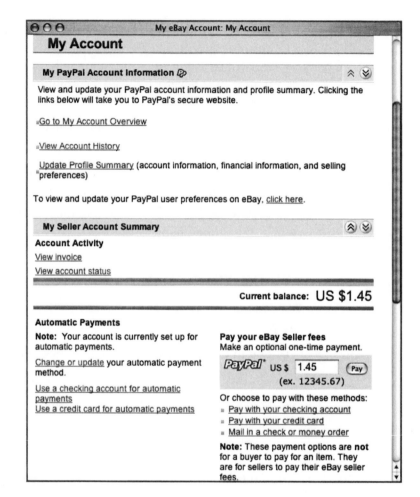

Figure 9.15

You can quickly and
simply check and pay your
balance all from the
same dashboard in the
My Account section
of My eBay.

3. Under Automatic Payment Method, select either Credit Card or
Checking Account to establish your preferences. Click Set Up
Automatic Payment.

4. Enter your credit-card or checking-account information, as shown in
Figure 9.16, and click Submit. The account you've selected will be
used from now on to automatically pay your seller's fees.

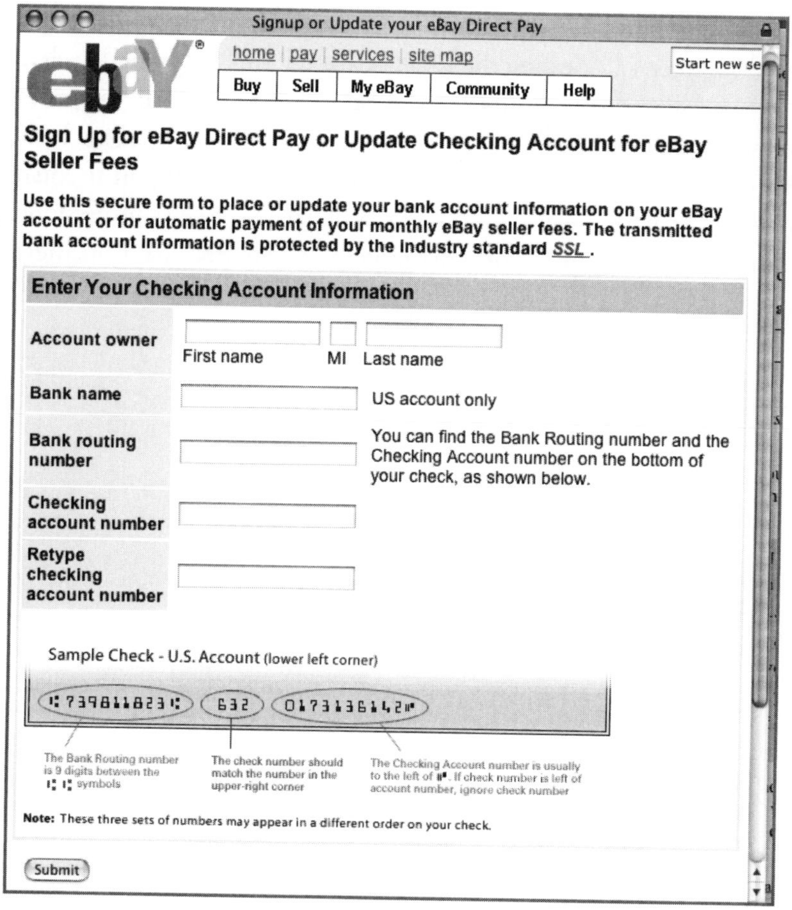

Figure 9.16

Enter your checking-account or credit-card information to have your seller's fees automatically deducted every month.

The Rest of the Story

Although the process of posting an auction is fairly simple, posting strategies require more knowledge. After all, just like a retail store or any other business, you're competing against many other sellers—some who have been doing this for several years—and need to find a way to gain the competitive edge. Also, as a seller of jewelry and watches, you must fully comprehend your obligations when writing an auction description, shipping and insuring, and performing other steps of the auction process. Otherwise, you could end up with some unhappy customers—or worse yet, have your listings pulled off eBay.

Chapter 11, "Creating Compelling—and Legally Correct—Product Descriptions," Chapter 12, "Sealing the Deal," Chapter 13, "Shipping Jewelry," and Chapter 14, "Protecting Yourself as a Seller" deal with all the rules, opportunities, and sales strategies that go into selling jewelry on eBay. First, however, I'll talk in the next chapter about how eBay can help you if you're already selling jewelry in the "real" world—that is, if you're a jewelry professional curious about how this intriguing online marketplace can help your business.

chapter 10

eBay for the Jewelry Professional

If you have been in the jewelry business for some time, eBay could answer a few of your lingering prayers. Whether you own a retail store for fine jewelry and watches, create and sell your own artisan designs, or operate a manufacturing facility for mass merchandise, there's inevitably some challenge, major or minor, that you face regularly. You are looking for new customers. You have had the same merchandise sitting in that corner case too long. Or you produced thousands of a certain style of necklace before realizing that it went out of style three years ago.

Luckily, eBay is so diverse that it can most likely meet just about any need you have. It can become everything from a dependable standby if you need to offload goods quickly, to a regular sales channel to boost your profits.

How Professionals Use It

eBay's Jewelry & Watches category is one of the few where quite a bit of the merchandise is *not* pre-owned. According to eBay, it's also a category that has a higher percentage of professionals—especially jewelry manufacturers and wholesalers—selling in it. So how has eBay found its place in the jewelry profession? The following is a partial list of how jewelers and others in the industry are using the site:

■ **Old stock or overstock.** Like most retailers, jewelry stores have a percentage of merchandise that just never sells. It sits in the case or the back room season after season, until the staff is sick of looking at it. But unlike department stores or other kinds of retail outlets, jewelry stores—especially those that have a high-brow reputation—are less likely to have a clearance sale to move their musty old jewelry. This is where eBay can come in. It's a fast, and probably more profitable, way to sell the nonmovers. Similarly, jewelry manufacturers might produce more of a certain piece in a single production cycle, and then need to move out the stuff that didn't sell before the new season of goods hit the production line. This is why you often might see multiple items that look similar. A manufacturer may have overproduced a style of hinged-hoop earrings, and then failed to sell the last 15 percent, so now he's selling them on eBay. Or a supplier might have imported too many goods and is going on his next buying trip to Hong Kong, so he needs to clear out space for the new products.

■ **Closeouts and liquidations.** As is the case in many industries, certain companies specialize in buying up the discontinued lines of suppliers and manufacturers, or in purchasing the remaining inventory of stores or companies that are going out of business. Occasionally, these closeout and liquidation companies will show up at jewelry industry events to sell the jewelry to other professionals for next to nothing. But with eBay, closeout merchants can skip the middleman and go straight to the consumer with their jewelry, which makes the prices even lower and the buy more attractive.

■ **Trade-ups for loyal customers.** Retail jewelers are often in the business of making a customer for life. So sometimes they'll try to make it easier for their customers to "trade in" their existing jewelry for higher-value pieces, much in the same way a car consumer trades up for a new car. These jewelers offer a discount to the customer in exchange for their used jewelry, and then they sell the old jewelry on eBay to make their money back.

■ **"Preloved" jewelry.** Some collectors and dealers of antique and estate jewelry, such as the jewelry shown in Figure 10.1, use eBay as one of their main channels to sell their wares. These can be people who have a very small storefront or none at all, or who use stalls at antique markets or gift marts as their primary face to the world, so eBay provides a wider audience with less overhead. Because the markup doesn't tend to be as high on antique and estate jewelry, dealers can often command prices from their eBay auctions that are comparable to what they'd make on an in-person sale.

Figure 10.1

eBay has earned a reputation as the place to go for bargains on "preloved" goods, and jewelry is no different. Sellers can do a big business in antique and estate fine jewelry and watches, as well as vintage costume jewelry, on eBay.

- **Wholesale to the public.** Every smart consumer loves hearing these four words, and wholesalers who specialize in that kind of thing know it. So wholesalers who import or buy jewelry and then sell it directly to consumers can have a field day with eBay, the perfect place to unload jewelry at prices well below retail.

- **Publicity for designers.** Because eBay is full of avid collectors, some fine and artisan jewelry designers use the site as a way to build a following for their latest creations. eBay can be used to hold over designers between exhibits at art or jewelry shows, drive traffic to their e-commerce Web sites, or build name recognition for designers trying to break into the business.

- **Purchasing materials.** Jewelry manufacturers and designers have found eBay to be an excellent source for buying gemstones, findings (clasps, wire, links, and the like), beads, and other raw materials for making their creations at good prices.

Who's Buying Jewelry on eBay?

In early 2004, the Jewelry Consumer Opinion Council (JCOC) conducted a survey of more than 2,000 jewelry shoppers to find out more about who was shopping on eBay. Of those surveyed, slightly more than 20 percent had purchased jewelry on eBay. Among that population, nearly 71 percent had purchased jewelry more than once, and more than 41 percent purchased only fine jewelry.

Profile of an eBay Jewelry Shopper

So who are these buyers? The JCOC's survey (see Figure 10.2) painted a picture of an eBay jewelry shopper who is

- Female (82.37 percent)
- 31 to 50 years old (53.32 percent)
- College-educated (62.75 percent had at least some college or a college degree)
- Married (60.71 percent)
- White (86.02 percent)
- Middle-class (44.02 percent had incomes between $35,000 and $75,000 a year)

Shopping Habits

The study also revealed what, and how, the consumers who purchase jewelry on eBay are buying—and the results are surprising and encouraging for would-be jewelry sellers. More than 41 percent of the group reported they shopped exclusively for fine jewelry, and nearly 50 percent are looking for unique styles (as opposed to discount, closeout, or brand-name items). About 23 percent tend to shop for rings, followed by bracelets and earrings as the most popular jewelry types. And more than 22 percent said they shopped for jewelry on eBay because of the convenience.

Interestingly, although shoppers are searching for unique, fine jewelry, the price points in which they shop indicate they're still looking for bargains. While 40 percent of respondents said they spent on average more than $50 on jewelry from eBay, the percentage fell dramatically for prices above $500.

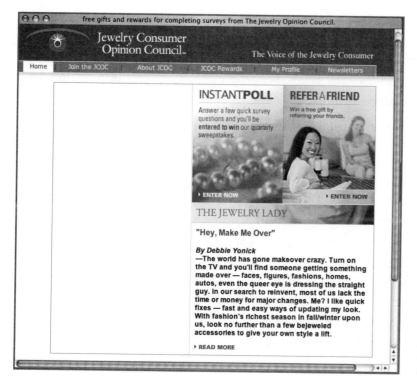

Figure 10.2

The Jewelry Consumer Opinion
Council surveyed jewelry
shoppers to learn who bought
on eBay and what those
shoppers' habits were.

There also appeared to be a clear preference toward purchasing from individuals (more than 60 percent). That's not to say that these bidders were *not* actually buying from an eBayer who was actually a manufacturer or retailer. Instead, the buyers responded that they felt they often dealt directly with an individual rather than a company—a major indicator that sellers should keep the personal touch alive in their interactions with buyers.

eBay and Perceived Value

Selling fine jewelry and watches is a tricky game, whatever the sales channel. Fine jewelry is a category that, for ages, has been marked with a sense of exclusivity, and keeping that aura is crucial to jewelers' ability to keep selling. Jewelry sellers promote the beauty and rarity of beautiful gems and metals, and the miracle of nature behind them, to build their value, but they also play up the heritage of jewels—the fact that jewels have been associated with royalty, celebrity, and wealth through the centuries—as well as their emotional value. That's why the diamond company De Beers has long promoted the artificial formula of "three months' salary" as a proper price for an engagement ring. The harder the jewelry is to attain, the more valuable it will seem in consumers' eyes.

Since the onset of mass merchandise and vehicles such as the home-shopping network QVC, the jewelry industry has struggled with the dilemma of how to maintain fine jewelry's value while still meeting the growing demands of consumers for more democratic product offerings. One example is Tiffany & Co., which decided several years ago to begin selling a line of well-designed sterling silver jewelry. Suddenly, a Tiffany locket or bracelet was attainable for a whole new level of consumer—younger shoppers with perhaps less disposable income than Tiffany's traditional customers. Although this gave Tiffany a chance to expand its brand and build new long-term customers, some argued that it took the extra shine off Tiffany's reputation. The store was no longer the place where Holly Golightly would look longingly into the front window while munching her morning croissant. Now, Holly could march right in and buy something much more substantial than a silver swizzle stick.

This is one dilemma with eBay. When asked about their perception of jewelry on eBay, the respondents of the JCOC survey were mixed. About 20 percent of consumers said they thought of the items as low quality, and nearly 16 percent believed that many items were knock-offs. On the other hand, 15.55 percent said they believed eBay offered a good variety and selection.

Does that mean that, as a jewelry retailer, wholesaler, or manufacturer, you run the risk of eroding your products' value by offering them on eBay? Not necessarily. In this day and age, more venerable institutions are trying to shed their formidable images in order to attract buyers who appreciate beauty—but might not be able to pay as much for it. "Some of these stores that have built strong brands are having to readjust their approach because they're scaring people off," says eBay's director of Jewelry & Watches Ann Poletti. She likens the dilemma to a similar one in the opera world: "The Met in New York always charged upwards of $150 for seats, but then they couldn't sell tickets. Now they offer $25 seats for part of the theater. They've learned that they can't intimidate people."

eBay is a way for sellers to bridge many different boundaries, not the least of which is geographic. "If a person lives in the Midwest, she might live two hours from an airport and further than that from a major city," Poletti says. "She might never get to a department store." And, where jewelry is concerned, eBay is a way for buyers to find unique items without knowing somebody "in the business." Poletti notes, "They have an equal shot at getting a great quality, unique item."

The truth is that today's consumer appreciates a more democratic approach to consumer goods. And even shoppers who do have the money to buy expensive items don't necessarily want to spend their money that way. The book *The Millionaire Next Door* by Thomas J. Stanley and William D. Danko, for example, profiled a new kind of wealthy consumer, one who still hunts for bargains, counts her pennies, and lives below her means. Although she still might seek a way to express herself through beautiful jewelry, she might very well shop eBay, rather than Manhattan's Fifth Avenue, for that special piece.

The eBay "Time Suck"

As a professional, you probably already have your hands full managing your business. Before you decide to charge into selling on eBay, you'll need to understand the time commitment it requires. Depending on how many items you're selling, eBay can quickly become a full-time job. If you want to make eBay a legitimate part of your business, you should prepare for this and dedicate the necessary resources.

Part-time sellers say they spend anywhere from four or five to more than 20 hours a week managing their auctions—and full-time sellers can spend between 40 and 60 hours. Selling involves more than just watching bids and waiting for an auction to close. Here are some of the other time-consuming duties that are required of you in order to become a credible seller:

- Writing auction descriptions
- Photographing items
- Answering bidders' questions

- Investigating bidder profiles and feedback

- Sending invoices

- Tracking and processing payments

- Packing items for shipping

- Taking packages to the Post Office, or scheduling courier pick-ups

- Tracking shipments

- Submitting feedback

Although some of these tasks seem simple enough, the time they take you can easily add up. That's why, if you're counting on eBay to grow into an important tool for your company, you might consider options for help. Some businesses actually dedicate a part- or full-time employee exclusively to the task of managing eBay auctions. At the very least, you should investigate tools to help you more efficiently manage your listings. See Chapter 12, "Sealing the Deal," for more information about these resources.

chapter 11

Creating Compelling—
and Legally Correct—
Product Descriptions

As the title of this chapter suggests, there are two equally weighted considerations when you set out to create your auction description. Foremost, you want to stand out from the crowd, attract attention, and inspire buyers to place a bid on your item. That's the fun part. Just as important, however, is that you must be sure you are following a few rules when it comes to representation and disclosure about your piece. To put it simply, this chapter covers the dos and don'ts of selling jewelry on eBay—and they're not necessarily self-explanatory. If you're looking to become a member of the jewelry sellers' community on eBay, don't skip this chapter!

Writing Descriptions That Sell

First, let's talk about the enjoyable part. You're lucky, really, because you've selected one of the most beautiful and romantic products about which you can write. A CD player or a cordless drill is probably not much fun to describe. With jewelry, however, you can use your imagination with your item descriptions—and the more imaginative you are, the more your bidders will fall in love with your items.

In this section, I'll first discuss some of the strategies you can take with the actual *content* of your descriptions. Then, I'll share a few tips about formatting, which can make or break even the strongest auction listing.

Content Strategies

With thousands of other auctions in the Jewelry & Watches category, you want to make sure your listing gets noticed. Consider a few of the following ideas for creating the best possible item description:

Tip

You might want to read a few descriptions written by PowerSellers in your category before you try to write a description of your own. That said, *do not* steal their words. This research should help you with strategy and inspiration only. Use your own creativity to conjure up the perfect description.

- **Provide as much detail as possible.** What do you know about the ring you're selling besides that it's made of gold and has three emeralds in it? Include all facts: carat weight, metal weight, age or era if you know it, design style, descriptions of interesting details (such as filigree, granulation, or other handwork), ring sizes, and gem grades.

- **Describe the visual appearance of the piece.** Photos usually don't do jewelry justice, especially when they're from a digital camera and posted on a Web site. Indulge in a little wordplay, using lush adjectives and emotional impressions of the piece.

- **Write for search engines.** Many buyers use the eBay search engine to search for keywords and terms that appear in an item description, not just the headline. So try to use terms and phrases that buyers will most likely use to search. This might require a little research on your part. Try looking at other items that are similar in style to the jewelry you're selling and gleaning popular terminology from them.

- **Educate your buyer.** Jewelry buyers, particularly those who are inexperienced, appreciate sellers who share their knowledge. Consider sharing a short primer on how to buy diamonds (see Figure 11.1), how to shop for vintage jewelry, or other background information. It will signal to your bidders that you know what you're doing and will also help them feel more at ease.

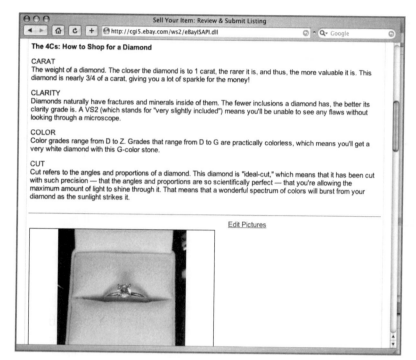

Figure 11.1

Some sellers include primers such as the 4Cs of how to buy diamonds in their auction description.

- **Include illustrations.** Support your description with well-constructed photographs of your item (see the section on jewelry photography later in this chapter) and, if you have them, scanned images of gem certificates, appraisals, or other documentation.

- **Write an About Me profile.** Buyers want to know more about you as an individual, so they feel comfortable buying from you. Use your About Me page to talk about your background selling jewelry, your business, your interests, or any other information you can share to create a personal connection between you and the buyer.

Formatting Hints

Sometimes auction sellers get carried away with all the formatting options they have at their disposal. As you build your auction listing, exercise discretion and err toward simplicity and readability with your formatting. Here are a few tips to keep in mind:

■ **Write for the Web.** People read differently on the Web than they do in print. They tend to skim text, and because of the flickering monitor, the eye has a more difficult time following large blocks of text. So use short sentences, and break your description up into brief paragraphs. Also use headers and bullets to further "chunk" your text into digestible pieces.

■ **Use emphasis strategically.** If you bold or italicize everything, nothing will stand out at all. Save your bold, italic, underline, or other formatting to highlight the most important things about your auction— the features that set you apart from the crowd.

■ **Avoid all caps.** As shown in Figure 11.2, words typed in all capital letters are impossible to read quickly, especially on the Web. In addition, many people see using all caps as the Internet equivalent of screaming, and may be turned off.

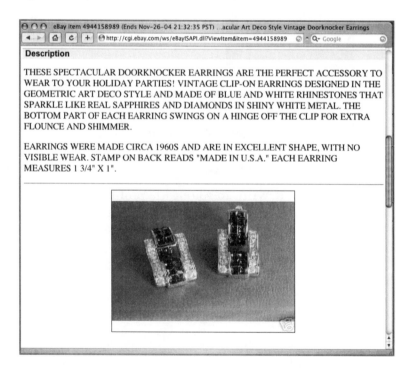

Figure 11.2

All caps, all the time, make auction descriptions impossible to read.

■ **Make sure the text is readable.** If you decide to use a background pattern or color, ensure that your text is in clear contrast to the background. Also use a font size that's large enough so people with less than 20/20 vision can read it (but not *too* large, of course). If you use eBay's Standard template (which allows you to enter text as you would in a word-processing program such as Microsoft Word), a font size of 10 or 12 should be fine. If you use the HTML template (which allows you to add HTML tags to format text), use a font size of 2.

■ **Check your spelling and grammar carefully.** Using correct grammar and spelling is always important, but even more so when selling a high-dollar product like jewelry. Buyers want to know they can trust you, so they'll be looking for clues as to your level of professionalism —and attention to detail is part of that. After all, how can you be trusted to guarantee the color and clarity of a diamond, standards that require a keen eye and deep knowledge, if you can't even string a sentence together? Proofread your listing word-for-word before posting it. If you're unsure about a word, look it up in the dictionary. Sometimes it even helps to read the listing out loud, to ensure it sounds as good as it looks on the screen.

Writing Law-Abiding Auction Descriptions

When I talk about law, I'm referring to two different systems: eBay law and real—federal and local—law. As an eBay seller, you are obligated to obey both legal systems—or else. Of course, depending on which system you violate, your error could result in a simple scolding to major fines and possible legal action. So be sure you understand what you can and can't do before posting your first auction description.

The FTC Guidelines

In 1996, the Federal Trade Commission published revisions to its guidelines for the jewelry industry on how to fairly sell goods. These guidelines were the most thorough, and widely applicable, set of rules for jewelry sellers in history. Before them, merchants were accountable to their city or state consumer protection laws, which were often vague and unfamiliar. But when the new guidelines were released, they were backed by the promise—from the FTC, local law enforcement agencies, and jewelry industry vigilance groups—that they would be strictly imposed.

What was the big deal about these guidelines? For one thing, a federal agency was mandating for the first time ever that jewelry and gemstone sellers across the United States had to disclose possible gemstone treatments, such as clarity enhancement, which until then had been virtually unrecognized in discussions with consumers.

The guidelines also cracked down on misrepresentation. Lab-created gemstones could no longer be classified as natural stones, and "imposter" jewels could no longer be described using the same terms as the real thing. The guidelines created a ripple throughout the jewelry industry, but through years of education, many offline jewelry merchants learned to comply with them, convinced that they would repair the industry's reputation for fairness and honesty.

For many years after these rules were imposed on the rest of the industry, misrepresentation continued to run rampant on eBay. Sellers who were either ignorant of or indifferent to the guidelines continued to describe CZ as diamonds, never disclosed treatments or lab-created gemstones, and generally created a snakepit for buyers looking for honest deals.

Not surprisingly, professional sellers who knew the difference and who upheld the guidelines in their own sales began complaining vociferously to eBay about their less-than-honest counterparts, who, they argued, were ruining eBay for the rest of the community. Working closely with these advocates, as well as with jewelry industry groups and the FTC, eBay stepped in to resolve the issues. In late 2004, eBay made a rare move when it announced it would become actively involved in monitoring the Jewelry & Watches category for compliance with the FTC guidelines. Any sellers who violated the guidelines, eBay proclaimed, would be subject to removal from the site. eBay set up a team of police to comb the site for such deceptive listings and pull them down if necessary. The company also relies on the help of eBay jewelry community members, who have become vigilantes to protect honest selling over the years and actively monitor and report deceptive listings.

A Brief Summary of the FTC Guidelines

As an eBay jewelry seller you need to understand your limits when describing an item in your auction listing. Following are the guidelines in a nutshell (for the complete publication, visit http://www.ftc.gov/bcp/guides/jewel-gd.htm):

- **Misuse of terms.** It's easy to get carried away when you're describing a gemstone or piece of jewelry. In your eyes, the piece is a miracle of beauty. But you must choose your words wisely. In the jewelry business, you have to mean exactly what you say. Table 11.1 sorts out the major no-nos of labeling jewelry.

Table 11.1 Using Jewelry Terms

You Are Prohibited from Using the Term...	Unless the Item...
Brilliant-cut diamond	Is a round diamond with at least 32 facets above the girdle and at least 24 facets below the girdle
Cultured pearl	Was cultured in salt or fresh water through the insertion of a bead into a mollusk
Diamond	Is a natural mineral consisting mostly of pure carbon, with a hardness of 10, a specific gravity of 3.52, and a refractive index of 2.42
Faux pearl	Is also called "artificial" or "imitation" in the description
Flawless or perfect	Truly has no blemishes, inclusions, inferior colors, or other flaws
Gemstone (and names of specific gemstones)	Is a gemstone that developed in nature, unless the immediately preceded by a term such as "lab-created," "laboratory-grown," "synthetic," or "imitation"
Gold (without a karatage)	Is solid 24-karat gold
Gold (with karatage)	Is a gold alloy with at least 10-karat gold in fineness
Hand-made or hand-polished	Was manufactured or polished using only manual processes and no machinery
Pearl, natural pearl, or natura pearl	Was created by a mollusk under "abnormal physiological conditions" and not interference from humans
Platinum	Is at least 950/1000th pure platinum
Precious or semiprecious	Was created in nature under natural conditions
Real, natural, or genuine	Was created in nature under natural conditions
Silver or sterling silver	Is at least 925/1000th pure silver
South Sea pearl	Originated from mollusks in the waters of the South Sea islands, Australia, or Southeast Asia

Some sellers might find these rules confining when trying to create their enticing auction headlines. It's tempting, for example, to describe that piece of costume jewelry with the deeply red rhinestones as an "exquisite ruby red bracelet." But according to the FTC guidelines, this is illegal because it is misleading. Your item description will need to be something more along the lines of "imitation ruby bracelet" or "deep red rhinestone bracelet."

■ **Disclosure of treatments.** This is the part of the FTC guidelines that's harder to understand and interpret. And not just for beginners: not unlike how judges try to uphold the original intentions of law-makers for a government's judicial system, industry leaders have been debating for years on the best way to read and implement the guide-lines. The problem is that nobody wants to put himself at risk, but at the same time, *overdisclosing* can be bad for business, because jewelers who talk about every standard treatment are probably shedding nega-tive light unnecessarily on the goods they're selling. A good rule of thumb is that you're required to disclose treatments if they might be reversible, if they require special care, or if they significantly reduce the value of the gemstone. Based on these guidelines, you should disclose the following treatments to your bidders:

■ Clarity enhancement that might require special care (such as fracture filling)

■ Dyeing or bleaching

This gets tricky if, as a seller, you're not aware that the gemstone has been enhanced. The person who sold it to you possibly didn't know or didn't tell you. Try to ask as many questions as possible about gemstone enhancements before you purchase from your source. Again, you needn't worry about standard enhancements such as heat treatments or irradiation, but clarity enhancement, dyeing, bleaching, or any other enhancement that suggests a stone is of lower value than it looks should be noted.

Tip

If you're relatively new to jewelry selling or aren't familiar with gemstone treatments, visit the American Gem Trade Association Web site at http://www.agta.org/consumer/gemstones/enhancements.htm to read about common treatments.

- **How to disclose.** Many sellers worry that discussing gemstone treatments in their auction descriptions might turn buyers off. This is where education, a different perspective, and a little creativity come in handy. The AGTA Web site can give you a few ideas on how to explain enhancements so that buyers understand they are common and safe. Approach them in your description positively, as a way of providing the world beautiful gemstones at affordable prices. Here's an example of how you might bring up heat treatment for a clarity-enhanced diamond:

> *The center stone in this lovely ring is a 2.30-carat, clarity-enhanced diamond, with a naturally beautiful E color. So that you can buy the most beautiful diamond at the best possible price, the diamond has undergone a technological process called fracture-filling, which hides the minor inclusions that occur naturally in some diamonds, thereby upgrading the clarity grade by a few levels. This safe enhancement creates a bright, clean, gorgeous diamond that you'll treasure forever!*

Although disclosure can seem somewhat disruptive, you can also view it as a small part of the gemstone's story—its journey from the earth to your buyer's mailbox.

Obeying the eBay Laws

eBay has established consumer protection rules that the FTC guidelines don't cover. Specifically, many of these rules prevent you from dishonestly linking your item with something it really isn't. This is only a partial list of rules. See http://pages.ebay.com/help/policies/listing-ov.html for a more comprehensive list.

- **Keyword spamming.** You are prohibited from using words in your title and description that will cause your listing to show up when buyers search for other types of items. In other words, you can't use the term "diamond" if you're really selling Austrian crystal, just because you want to attract more potential buyers to the listing.

- **Brand-name misuse and illegal comparisons.** You cannot use a brand name or trademark unless it describes the manufacturer or brand of the item you're actually selling. Calling a piece "Tiffany-like" or "Bulgari style" in your headline is deemed misleading by eBay and violates the rules. Even if you do see auctions like this on the site frequently, eBay's published rule is that these comparisons are illegal, and that auctions that use these kinds of comparisons or use brand names that don't belong to them will be pulled off the site.

Photographing Jewelry for Auctions

Photographs are vital to the success of any auction. Especially in the Jewelry & Watches category, beautiful photographs are essential to driving demand for your items. Rich colors, close-ups of details, and proof of trademarks and other distinguishing characteristics are the best testaments that your item is as gorgeous as you say it is.

Doing justice to a beautiful piece of jewelry is tricky for amateur photographers —which is what most of us are—who don't have the best equipment and a professional studio. However, there a few tricks you can use to get the best possible image, spending only a few dollars to establish a makeshift set-up.

What You Need

This section outlines what equipment you need to create photographs that will entice browsers to bid on your piece:

- **Digital camera.** If you hope to sell a lot of merchandise on eBay, consider investing in a decent digital camera. You're going to be taking a lot of pictures, and using a digital camera is much easier and faster—not to mention cheaper—than running film over to the photo-developing counter every other day. These days, you can purchase a perfectly fine-quality, name-brand one for about $150 to $250. For your purposes, you're going to need something that:

  - Is at least 2.1 megapixels for sharp, good-quality photos

  - Has a macro or close-up setting (usually designated by a tulip symbol)

  - Allows you to turn off the flash

  - Has a timer

- **Tripod.** Close-up photography requires a steady camera. No matter how still you think you're being, the imperceptible movement of your hands will cause the shot to blur. You can buy a very cheap tripod on eBay (mine was $3.99) that screws into the bottom of your camera and bends to angle your camera toward the shot.

- **Macro lens.** You can purchase a macro lens that lets you get even closer to your subject—about 3 inches away versus the 6 inches you can feasibly shoot from with your regular lens. Check your user guide for your camera to find out which size lens your camera supports. You can also find these on eBay or other discount camera Web sites. The macro lens is not a necessity, but it does help you offer your bidders the best, most detailed visual representation of your product.

- **Stands, platforms, and props.** To give your jewelry life, you will want it to be propped or hung from something, which is where jewelry stands come in handy. On the other hand, some sellers prefer to lay the jewelry flat on a surface that provides a bit of a reflection, or to use a background that has texture to make the composition of the photo more interesting. You can also use putty, wax, or another substance that cleans off easily and can be hidden to keep items in place while you capture the perfect shot. Your own approach will take some experimentation, but you can find all the materials you need on eBay or other Web sites.

- **Photography tent or tabletop studio.** Jewelry photography requires a certain approach to lighting, so you'll need to find a "tent" or table-top studio to get the lighting just right. This is actually easier than it sounds. Some people purchase branded tabletop studios such as EZcube. However, making your own tent works just as well. I use a 19-quart, rectangular plastic box made by Rubbermaid. Turn it on its side and place the jewelry inside it, and the translucent plastic provides good diffusion for the light shining through it. I'll talk about why this is important in a minute.

- **Lighting.** Jewelry looks best in light that's as close as possible to natural light, or sunlight, which emits a cooler tone than your average incandescent light bulb in a household lamp. Luckily, a brand new type of light bulb has hit the market recently that can help you out. Philips and GE both now make daylight or natural light bulbs, which are whiter, cooler lights than traditional soft light bulbs. This light will help illuminate your jewelry and make it sparkle.

You might also want to invest in either three small desk lamps or three clip-on lamps, which you can find at a discount store for under $10 apiece. And finally, keep some wax paper, a white plastic bag, or a piece of Mylar that you can hang over one of your lights—preferably something that won't catch on fire if it gets hot!

Snapping the Picture

When it comes to taking the actual photo, follow these directions for capturing the perfect shot.

1. Set up your photography tent or tabletop studio. Place your jewelry inside, propped up slightly so you can get a good angle to shoot it directly.

2. Place one light on each side of the tent, so the light shines through the sides of the tent. This diffused light illuminates the jewelry brightly but subtly, with fewer harsh shadows.

3. Hang your piece of wax paper, plastic, or Mylar over the front of the third light. Position this light directly in front of the tent, shining right at the jewelry. This is the diffused light that will create the sparkle in your stones and metal. Figure 11.3 shows how the setup should look.

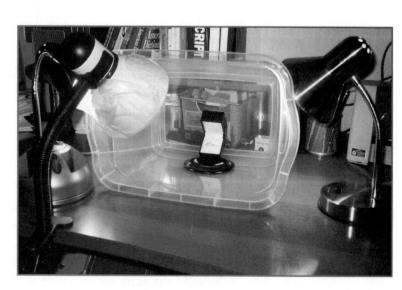

Figure 11.3

Set up your jewelry inside a makeshift jewelry tent— in this case, a Rubbermaid box turned on its side—and position three lights to shine on the jewelry at different angles for the best lighting effect.

4. Turn your camera on. Using your settings, turn *off* your flash and turn *on* your macro setting (read your user guide for help).

5. Position your camera on a tripod or stand (even a stack of books will suffice) about six inches from your jewelry (unless you have a macro lens, in which case you can get a couple inches closer).

6. Set up your shot using your LCD monitor rather than your optical viewfinder. (When you're shooting from this close, you will experience something called *parallax*, where your viewfinder and lens are in different places. If you use the viewfinder, your subject will be offset in the shot, but your monitor can help resolve that.)

7. Prefocus your shot. Usually, you can do this by pressing down halfway on your shutter button.

8. Set your timer, press the shutter button, and stand back to wait for the shot to snap.

Editing Your Image

Even after you've carefully set up your lighting and shot, you will inevitably need to correct the color and brightness in your image. Photo-editing software can help you with this. Plug your camera into your computer and upload your image. Then open the image in your photo-editing software. There is an auto correction or auto levels function in most software that will automatically adjust your color tone, brightness, and contrast.

If you don't already own an expensive software package such as Adobe Photoshop, there's no need to purchase a professional package just to edit images for eBay. Instead, look for free or more affordable software. A few of the free ones available include VCW Vicman's Photo Editor (http://www.vicman .net/vcwphoto) and Serif PhotoPlus (http://www.freeserifsoftware.com). If you're going to be taking and editing a lot of images, however, it might be worthwhile to invest in a software program that gives you more options and an easier, more professional interface. Adobe Photoshop Elements, a scaled-down version of Photoshop (see Figure 11.4), retails for around $90.

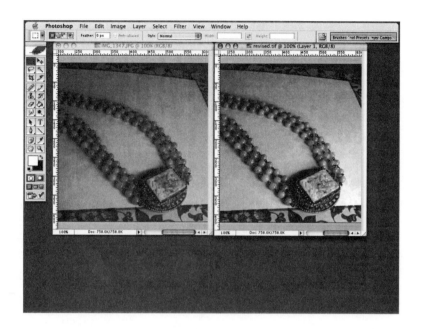

Figure 11.4

You can use photo-editing software to brighten and correct the tone of your jewelry photo. In this example, the original image (left) was dark and had a red tone to it. The Auto Levels feature in Adobe Photoshop Elements instantly brightened the picture and made it whiter (right) to better represent the color of the jewelry.

Now you've created an auction description—complete with a photo—that you can be proud of, and posted your auction. What's next? Waiting, watching, and hoping your hard work pays off. The next chapter helps you weather those excruciating first days while you're waiting for your first auction to end—and covers what happens when it finally does.

chapter 12

Sealing the Deal

Now the suspense begins. Will somebody bid on your jewelry? The first time you place an item up for sale, you'll most likely check its activity regularly, anxiously. You'll wait to see if the eBay community will take interest in your item—and in you as a seller. Selling almost becomes personal, as if you're seeking acceptance from the site's seasoned buyers and sellers.

But if your bid numbers don't shoot upward right away, don't feel defeated. Keep in mind that there is some science involved in getting goods to sell. Remember, you're competing with thousands of other products—not just jewelry, but other items in the same price range that could easily substitute as a gift or what have you. It might take some experimentation and tenacity to get your item sold. Don't give up if you don't have success the very first time! I'll talk in a moment about what happens if your item *doesn't* sell, and some of the techniques you can use to recalibrate your auction technique.

Watching Your Auction

You've listed your first auction, and for now all you should do is eagerly await your first bid. At this point, it's too early to think pessimistically! You can easily check your auction's activity by using My eBay. Just log in, click the My eBay tab, and you'll have access to all the information you need. As you see in Figure 12.1, My eBay shows you

- The current price
- The number of bids

- The number of users who have added the auction to their watched items lists

- The number of users who have sent you questions about the auction

- The user ID of the current high bidder

- The amount of time your auction has left—in days, hours, and minutes

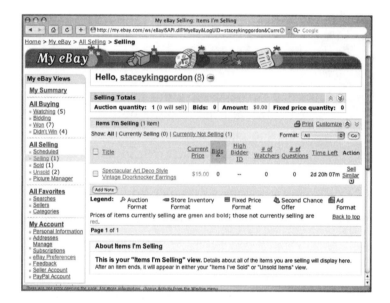

Figure 12.1

The status of your auctions is conveniently summed up in a simple dashboard on My eBay.

The header for the column showing the number of bids is a link. By clicking on it, you can drill down to see the user IDs of everyone who is bidding on your item, as well as their history. This will give you insight into who's competing for your item—information that will be especially interesting if you have two bidders duking it out as your price rises steadily higher.

Down the road, you might become such a busy seller with so many active auctions that you won't have time to monitor each of them obsessively. Your first few auctions, however, will be different. You'll find yourself checking in every hour on the hour to see if anybody has at the very least added the auction to her watched items list. And when you have five or seven days left before the end of the auction, it's hard to know what to do with yourself. In addition to remaining patient, there are a few things you can do to help your item sell successfully and safely.

Monitoring Your Buyers

You're probably curious about who your bidders are. More importantly, you may be concerned about their track records—have they bought from eBay in the past, and have they been on their best behavior? What kinds of items have they won? Are they mostly jewelry shoppers, or do they snap up shoes, vintage postcards, or old board games too? A buyer's bid history will tell you all of this.

Enforcing Policies

But what can you do with this information? What if, suddenly, you find a few bidders who appear to be up to no good—for example, they have miserably poor feedback themselves or a history of squabbling with their sellers—trawling your auction? Are you allowed to be choosy about who gets to bid on your item? Well, in fact, some sellers on eBay actually establish policies outlining the buyers with whom they prefer to do business. Some state that they refuse to sell to bidders with low or negative feedback, or they demand that those buyers contact them ahead of time before placing a bid. Others will not sell to buyers outside of their own geographical area—which is a rule that can be set when you create your auction listing.

If you are selling something that's very rare or valuable, you might want to establish a similar policy when you list your item. As explained in Chapter 9, "From Buyer to Seller," you want to set clear policies up front, *before* you encounter problems, and this is especially true if you plan to restrict bidding in any way. You must publish your bid-restriction policy clearly and prominently on every auction, as Figure 12.2 shows. Only then can you cancel bids from any bidders who don't measure up to your standards. For example, you might write a policy that stipulates the following:

- You'll cancel bids from buyers who have a feedback score of 0.

- You'll cancel bids from buyers who have received any negative feedback in the past 30 or 60 days.

- You require that buyers contact you in advance of placing a bid if they have low or negative feedback, or you will automatically cancel their bid.

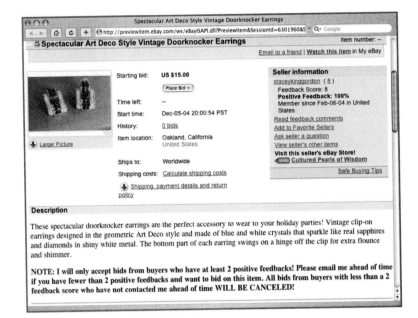

Figure 12.2

If you are selling an item that is particularly rare or valuable and you don't want to take your chances, you might want to establish clear policies upfront about which kinds of buyers you prefer and which you prohibit.

Caution

Of course, by enacting such a policy, you may alienate potential bidders. New buyers aren't necessarily dishonest or irresponsible—they're just discovering eBay for the first time. And buyers who have one or two negative feedback dings might not necessarily be bad eBayers. They might have just had run-ins with the wrong sellers.

Preapproving Buyers

If you like, you have the option of preapproving bidders. Similar to what the big, old-school auction houses do before they accept bids from potential buyers, this process involves asking buyers to register with you ahead of time in order to be placed on a list of permitted bidders. If you want to pre-approve bidders for your auction, you should state in your auction listing that you require prospective bidders to contact you before bidding in order to be added to a list of prequalified bidders. Then, if you're happy with what you see when you investigate a bidder's bid history and feedback, you can add that bidder's user ID to your list of preapproved buyers. To set up a preapproval list, do the following:

1. After you've posted an auction (and noted in the auction listing description that bidders must be preapproved), type http://pages.ebay .com/help/sell/preapprove_bidders.html in your Web browser address bar. Then click the link labeled "Start or edit a preapproved list."

2. Click the Add a new item with preapproved bidders link.

3. In the screen shown in Figure 12.3, type your auction item number.

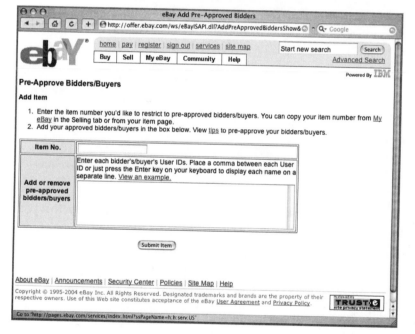

Figure 12.3

Once your auction is posted on eBay, you can add a list of preapproved buyers simply by entering the user IDs of bidders who have contacted you about participating.

4. Enter the user IDs of your preapproved bidders. Place a comma between multiple IDs, or press Enter or Return between IDs to list each on a new line. After you've added all the user IDs, click Submit Item.

5. To edit your preapproved bidders list, return to http://pages.ebay.com/ help/sell/preapprove_bidders.html at any time during the auction's duration, click the link labeled "Start or edit a pre-approved list," and click Edit beside the name of your auction (see Figure 12.4).

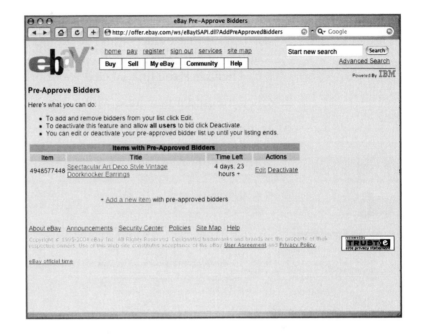

Now you have limited your bids to users who have signed up for your approval list. This kind of exclusive auction isn't for everybody, and I strongly caution you to use it only with items that are very rare, expensive, or unique. Otherwise, you could very well be setting yourself up for failure. Remember, the more bidders who take interest in your item, the higher your end price could be.

Note

If you find that requiring bidders to be preapproved is stemming the tide of prospective bidders, you can disable preapproval to open the auction back up to all users. Simply return to http://pages.ebay.com/help/sell/preapprove_bidders.html, click the link labeled "Start or edit a pre-approved list," and click Deactivate next to the name of your auction. Then click the Deactivate button to confirm.

Blocking Buyers Using eBay Preferences

So that you needn't monitor bids from buyers to make sure they meet your criteria, you can block buyers with certain characteristics. Your eBay Preferences allow you to block bids from users for whom at least one of the following pertains:

- They are located in countries to which you have not agreed to ship items.

- They have a feedback score below zero (−1, −2, or −3), which can happen when a buyer has more negative feedback than positive feedback.

- They've received two Unpaid Item strikes in the past 30 days.

- They don't have a PayPal account.

Tip

Again, to be completely fair, you should list the criteria by which you choose to block buyers in your auction description, so that bidders aren't caught off guard if their bid is blocked.

To set your preferences so that buyers who meet any of the above criteria are automatically blocked from bidding on your auctions, do the following:

1. Log in and go to My eBay.

2. From the left navigation bar, click eBay Preferences.

3. Scroll down to Seller Preferences. As shown in Figure 12.5, you should see a status of "No buyer blocks" next to the "Block buyers who" line. Click Change.

4. Check the boxes next to the blocks you wish to place on all auctions (now and going forward), as shown in Figure 12.6. Click Submit.

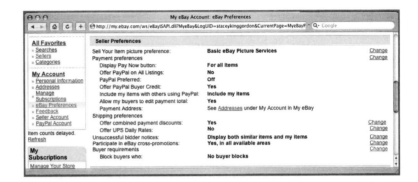

Figure 12.5

In your eBay Preferences, check to see if you currently have any automatic blocks on buyers. If not, click Change to place blocks.

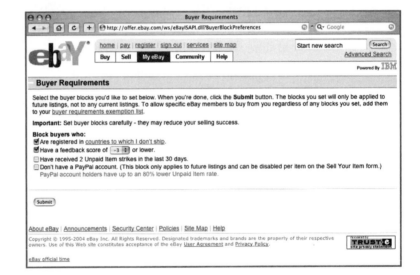

Figure 12.6

Mark as many check boxes as you wish to block certain buyers from bidding on your auctions.

Canceling a Bid

Only if you've publicized your policy restricting bids to buyers who meet your criteria do you have the right to cancel bids. Again, do so selectively—only if you have clearly posted your wishes about who can and can't bid, and only if you feel your bidder potentially poses a legitimate danger to you. To cancel a bid, do the following:

1. Type http://pages.ebay.com/help/sell/cancel_bids.html in your Web browser address bar.

2. Click the Cancel bids link.

3. In the screen shown in Figure 12.7, enter the item number of your auction.

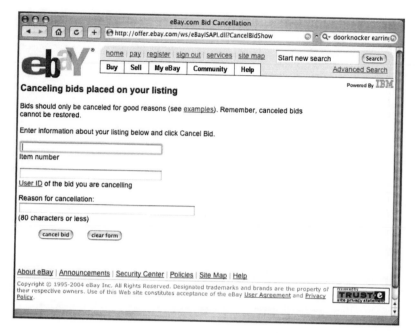

Figure 12.7

You're required to explain why you've decided to cancel any bids submitted by eBay users. eBay actually monitors all canceled bids and reviews the reasons behind them.

4. Enter the user ID of the bidder whose bid you're canceling.

5. In 80 words or less, write the reason you're canceling the bid. Reference your bid policy if you have one.

6. Click Cancel Bid. This will cancel every bid the buyer has submitted for this auction.

Next, in all fairness, you should send an e-mail message to the bidder letting her know you've canceled her bid.

Communicating with Your Buyers

While your auction is in play, buyers can send you messages asking you questions about the item, your selling and shipping policies, and other information. These messages will be sent to your primary e-mail account, but you can also read and manage these messages using My eBay. Just click Selling on the left navigation bar. The number of messages you've received will show up as a link on the row next to your auction listing. Click the link to see the messages and respond to them quickly using a message form, shown in Figure 12.8.

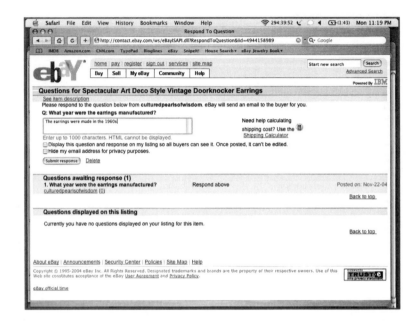

Figure 12.8

You can read and answer
questions from eBay buyers
easily using My eBay.

A mark of a good seller is your willingness and ability to respond to inquiries quickly. Buyers who ask a question and never hear back from you will most likely never place a bid, and will definitely never return for your other auctions in the future.

Caution

If someone e-mails you offering to buy your item outside of the auction channel, you are *not* allowed to accept. The only way an early sale is acceptable is if you offer a Buy It Now option, and the buyer selects that option before any other bids come in. If you do accept an unofficial offer to buy the product, you and the buyer are susceptible to suspension of your eBay user IDs.

Promoting Your Item

If you're a few days into your auction and you haven't had any luck—your page counter isn't showing many hits and nobody's watching your auction, let alone bidding on it—it's not too late to promote your item using one of eBay's promotional upgrades. See Chapter 9 for a list of the possible upgrades.

To promote your item in the middle of your auction, do the following:

1. Go to My eBay and click Selling on the left navigation bar.

2. Click the title of your auction.

3. At the top of your auction page, click the Promote Your Item link.

4. Check boxes next to the promotional upgrades you'd like to use.

5. Click Continue.

6. Review your upgrade and the associated fee, as seen in Figure 12.9, and then click Submit.

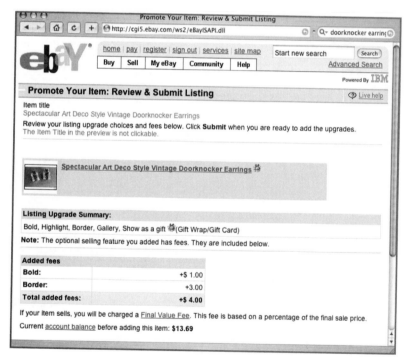

Figure 12.9

Before submitting your upgrade, you can preview the results and review the fee you'll be charged.

Editing Your Auction

eBay only allows you to change your auction title and description *before* you receive bids. After your first bid comes in, you need to leave your auction alone. But if you haven't attracted any visible attention from the auction in a couple of days, you might want to tinker with your keywords, description, photos, or even policies. To edit your auction, do the following:

1. Go to My eBay and click Selling from the left navigation bar.

2. Click the title of your auction.

3. At the top of your auction page, click Revise Your Item. Verify your item number and click Continue.

4. Each section of the auction that you're able to edit will have an Edit link next to it (labeled "Edit title," "Edit description," and so on), as shown in Figure 12.10. Click the link next to the section you want to edit.

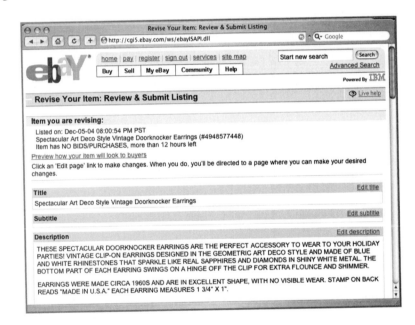

Figure 12.10

Click the Edit tag next to whichever section of your auction you want to revise—title, description, shipping, or payment information, for example.

5. Make your edits and click Save Changes.

Before you radically rewrite your auction listing, however, you should weigh the possibility that buyers might already be familiar with your auction. Even if no buyers have added your auction to their watch list, if the listing has been up for a few days, users may have stumbled upon it and it could be lingering in their minds, calling to them. If they decide to go looking for it again and you've changed the title or keywords within the description, however, your potential bidders might not be able to find it again. Remember that you've had a few days of publicity already, and although it's not immediately apparent to you, it's possible that your item has moved somebody.

eBay forbids you from editing the auction once a bid has been placed on it. That said, you are allowed to *add* to your item description using the editing process just outlined. Some sellers do so to provide answers to questions they've received from interested parties. You are also allowed to add a second category in which to list the auction—useful if you want to get more exposure for your listing.

The End of the Affair

It's not over 'til it's over, and the final minutes or seconds of your auction could hold some sweet surprises for you. After the dust has cleared and the header on the listing proclaims "Bidding has ended for this item," you either need to jump into action to wrap up the final details of the sale, or contend with what to do if your item hasn't sold.

If Your Item Didn't Sell...

First, don't be discouraged if your item didn't sell. Regular eBay sellers will tell you that it typically takes two or three listings before they get a bite. This is where software to help you automatically list and relist items will come in handy. I'll talk about those resources in Chapter 15, "Getting Serious About Selling." For now, you need to decide whether you want to relist your item at all, and if you do, what changes you'd like to make to your listing strategy. Here are a few things to consider:

■ **Time your auction just right.** If you select a seven-day auction format, for example, think about what's happening seven days from the exact moment you click Submit. Will it be early in the morning, when people are heading off to work? Will it be a Saturday afternoon, when people are out running errands? Or will it be a holiday, like Christmas or the Fourth of July, when everybody will be preoccupied with family? Because the heaviest bidding typically comes in the final hours and minutes of auctions, you'll want to time your auction to end during eBay's peak activity hours, usually nonholiday weekday evenings and Sundays.

- **Explore the site for similar items.** If there are a number of items in the same category that are very much like the one you're selling, you have some competition. You might want to wait until the other auctions end before you list yours again.

- **Get inspired by successful sales.** Now you'll want to search the site for similar items again, but this time look for auctions that are already closed. (See Chapter 2, "Doing Your Homework," for details on how to conduct an Advanced Search of completed items.) Read a few of the auctions that attracted several bids to get ideas about what the sellers did differently from you—how they wrote their titles and descriptions, how their photos look compared to yours, if their shipping or payment policies are radically different, or if they listed in different subcategories from you. If you see ideas you like, adapt them to your relisting—but be careful not to steal ideas outright. Don't copy titles or descriptions word-for-word, for example. Simply use the ideas to influence your own unique approach.

You can quickly and easily relist your item. Either go to the Unsold link on My eBay and click Relist next to the name of the unsold item, or go to the ended auction listing itself and click Relist at the top of the listing, as shown in Figure 12.11. You'll see a preview of the auction listing, with Edit links beside each section that will allow you make changes to your title, description, pricing, timing, and policies. Using the strategies outlined in this chapter, you can change the parts of the auction that you feel need strengthening rather than building a brand new auction listing from scratch. When you're finished with your edits, click Submit Listing. Relisting your item is *free* the first time you do it as long as you follow process I've just outlined.

If the Item Sold...

If you're lucky, you had at least one bid for your item that met any reserves you may have set, and an eBay buyer is now the lucky new owner of your jewelry treasure. Now what? Well, as the seller, it's your responsibility to make the first move by sending an invoice to the buyer, letting her know her next steps and obligations.

Figure 12.11

You can quickly relist your unsold item from My eBay or from the page for the ended auction.

After your auction has ended, you will immediately receive an e-mail from eBay notifying you of the final price and the winning bidder's user ID. As Figure 12.12 shows, you can click a button from within this e-mail to send an invoice to the winning bidder right away. Or, you can log in and go to My eBay later to send the invoice from there. Either way, an electronic invoice tallying the final price of the auction, your shipping costs, and any insurance you wish to add (if you give buyers the option of choosing insurance instead of making it mandatory in your policies) will be automatically created and e-mailed to the highest bidder. If you want, you can also send a separate e-mail to the buyer thanking her for her purchase and detailing your commitment to fast payment processing and shipping.

Now, you've made two solid efforts to proactively contact your buyer, so you should wait a couple of days for a reply. But what if you don't hear from your buyer in that time frame? After two or three days, if you haven't received payment, you should e-mail the buyer one more time, emphasizing that your buyer should contact you right away with a message about how she plans to pay. You might also suggest that you will relist the item if you don't hear from her within 24 to 48 hours. If you still don't hear back from the buyer, then it's time request her contact information through eBay. See Chapter 8, "The Good, the Bad, and the Ugly," for information on how to request contact information on an eBay user.

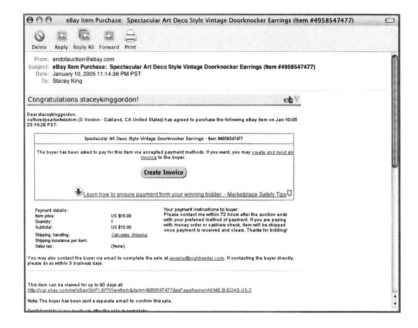

Figure 12.12

The easiest and fastest way to invoice your winning bidder is to click the button in the e-mail you receive from eBay, announcing the end of your auction.

Tip

Read more about how to deal with problem buyers in Chapter 14, "Protecting Yourself as a Seller."

Collecting Payment

For now, assume that your buyer, like most buyers, is an upstanding one. When she receives your invoice, she will use eBay's response system to notify you how she plans to pay. If you accept PayPal, she will most likely instantly authorize a PayPal payment to you. Or she will send you an eBay notification (or an e-mail) informing you that her check or money order is in the mail.

Tax Obligations

You have two things to consider when it comes to paying taxes on your eBay sales. First, you are obligated to pay federal and state income tax on your net income. In most cases, you'll need to report this income on a Schedule C along with your usual 1040 tax form. Then there's the somewhat confusing issue of state sales tax. Unless you live in a state that does not charge sales tax at all (Alaska, Florida, Nevada, South Dakota, Texas, Washington, and Wyoming), you must charge and pay sales tax if you sell to buyers in your own state. Rates vary by state; visit the Federation of Tax Administration's table of state sales tax rates at http://www.taxadmin.org/fta/rate/sales.html to look up rates in your own state.

Where it gets tricky is when you're selling an item to a buyer who *doesn't* live in your state (which, on eBay, will be most of the time). Although in the past, e-commerce vendors were not required to pay sales tax for selling goods across state lines, rules are starting to change. Many states are enacting legislation to streamline and regulate the collection of sales tax by Internet sellers, even those who are considered "remote" sellers. But these states vary in terms of how they are implementing and enforcing that legislation.

The problem is that it is illegal for you to collect sales tax if it isn't required by law, so you can't just tack on a few percentage points as a precautionary measure. The best thing to do is to find your state sales tax rules on the Internet to determine which rules apply to you. Using an Internet search engine, type the name of your state and the term "state tax department." This should point you to your state's tax administration board. If you still have questions, you should talk to a tax accountant.

PayPal Payments

If you have a PayPal account already, the buyer will be able to send a payment to you with the click of a button. You will receive an e-mail at the address you've registered with PayPal notifying you that a payment has been sent to you. As Figure 12.13 shows, this e-mail will contain a link that, when you click it, will open the PayPal site in a new browser window. You'll be prompted to log in to your account with the user ID and password you created back in Chapter 1, "Getting Started on eBay."

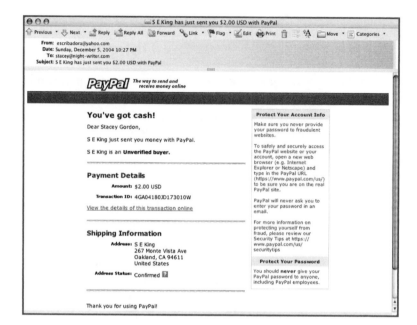

Figure 12.13

You'll receive a notification e-mail every time you receive a payment through PayPal.

Caution

If you're using a Personal PayPal account, which is what you signed up for in Chapter 1, you can only accept payments that have been funded by a buyer's bank account or existing PayPal funds. If a buyer places a credit card on file and uses it to pay you for the auction, you'll need to upgrade to a Premier PayPal account to accept the funds. You'll be given the option to upgrade when you sign in to accept the new funds. You get a few other extra perks with Premier, but the ability to accept credit and debit card–funded payments through PayPal is the biggest reason to upgrade, because many buyers pay using a credit card for security reasons. Note that you pay a small fee to receive money using a Premier PayPal account.

If you've received money from a buyer, you now have a few options. You can:

- Keep the money you've received for future use if you pay your own debts (from eBay or other services) using PayPal. The money you receive will be automatically added to your PayPal balance, and you can choose to use these funds when you send money to someone else later on.

■ Transfer money directly into your bank account (if you have a checking or savings account on file with PayPal), as you see in Figure 12.14. Simply click My Account, and then Transfer Funds to Your Bank Account. Enter the amount you want to transfer, select the bank account to which you want to send money, and click Continue. Then review the transaction and click Submit.

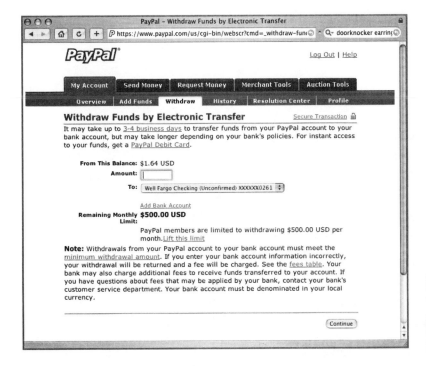

Figure 12.14

Your Premium PayPal account allows you to transfer your balance directly into your personal bank account.

■ You can request that PayPal issue you a paper check by mail, for a $1.50 fee.

■ You can use the balance you have to pay for any eBay purchases you're planning to make.

■ You can sign up for a number of PayPal-branded cash services, including debit cards and a money-market account backed by Barclays Global Fund Advisors.

Other Kinds of Payment

If you agreed to accept other kinds of payment beyond PayPal, it's possible that your buyer will elect to pay using one of those methods. These might include

- Other online payment services
- Personal or cashier's check
- Money order
- Bank-to-bank wire transfer
- Credit card (if you have a merchant account that allows you to accept credit cards)

Again, a buyer can't use any of these methods unless you selected them when setting up your payment terms when you listed your auction. And although PayPal is by far the easiest service to use, you might decide you don't want to pay PayPal's fees or feel squeamish about putting a credit card or bank account on file with the service. Or, you might want to leave the door open to make paying as convenient as possible for buyers and accept many different kinds of payments. Either way, here's a short primer on how you'll need to deal with each kind of payment.

- **Other online payment services.** Online payment services other than PayPal enable you to accept payments securely on the Web. Some, such as Yahoo! Pay Direct (http://paydirect.yahoo.com), work exactly the same way PayPal does—after you've established an account, you can have money paid to your account via an e-mail address. Others work a little differently. For example, Escrow.com, shown in Figure 12.15, allows buyers to send money to the service, which then holds the money in a trust account, verifies payment to the seller, and sends payment to the seller once the buyer receives the item. This system provides peace of mind for buyers and sellers alike. As a seller, you'll need to have accounts set up on any of these sites before you can start accepting payments through them.

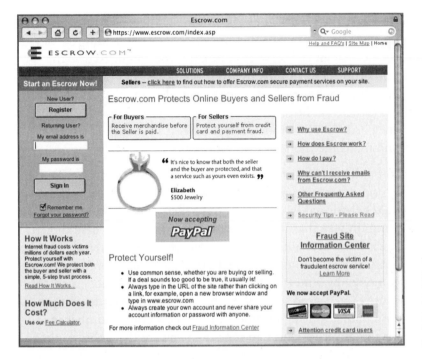

Figure 12.15

Escrow.com is an online payment service that provides an alternative to PayPal and offers an extra layer of security.

Caution

Buyers and sellers should beware when using escrow sites! Frightening as it may seem, there are dozens and dozens of fraudulent escrow sites online. The only site eBay endorses is Escrow.com, a legitimate, licensed escrow company. Any others are suspect, so do your homework and exercise caution before deciding to send your funds to the service for safekeeping.

■ **Checks.** Personal checks often take several days to clear, and your bank will probably charge you a hefty fee if they *don't* clear. You're probably safer accepting cashier's checks, which are checks issued directly by a bank after the face value of the check is paid to the bank by the payer. Either way, be sure to take the checks to your bank and find out your bank's policy on clearing checks before you ship your item.

- **Money orders.** Like cashier's checks, money orders are issued when a person pays the face value of the money order to an issuing agency, such a bank or financial services company. You might receive the money order in the mail directly from the buyer, or you might get it from an online money order service (a popular one is Western Union Auction Payments at http://www.auctionpayments.com, which collects the money order's value from a buyer's credit or debit card, then issues and mails the money order on the buyer's behalf).

- **Bank-to-bank wire transfer.** Wire transfers are out of favor these days on eBay and other auction sites, because they're unsafe for buyers who could get tricked by unscrupulous sellers (indeed, this is the most common way that buyers are tricked into sending cash directly out of their bank accounts, only to never receive their items). On the other hand, sometimes international buyers are most comfortable sending money by wire transfer rather than taking chances with the mail service. You'll need to provide the buyer with your banking institution name, routing number, and bank account number in order for the buyer to send you money. Be aware that most banks charge large fees for the privilege of accepting a wire transfer, especially an international one. Contact your bank for details about how wire transfers work with your account policy.

- **Credit cards.** If you are doing steady business on eBay, or if you sell through other channels and supplement your income with eBay, you might want to set up a credit-card merchant account, which allows you to take credit-card payments directly, rather than through PayPal. Most casual sellers don't do this because merchant accounts cost money; you usually have to pay the credit-card company a small fee or percentage for every transaction you process through the merchant account. You can usually get a merchant account through your regular bank or use one of the many services available on the Web for e-commerce merchants. In fact, even PayPal offers a merchant account that allows you to accept credit cards directly. Keep in mind as you shop around that rates vary, and so does reputation. You'll be better off going with a merchant account provider that you've heard of and trust.

Leaving Feedback for Your Buyer

Feedback is a bit of a game on eBay, and many times sellers will wait to see what a buyer says about them before they leave their own feedback for buyers. That's because many sellers see feedback as a tit-for-tat situation: If you scratch my back, I'll scratch yours. And because they're unable to retract feedback after they've submitted it, many sellers don't like the idea of bequeathing positive feedback, only to receive negative feedback in return. In my view, however, this is the *wrong* way to approach feedback. If a buyer pays quickly and efficiently and is a solid communicator, you are obligated to leave positive feedback as soon as the deal is done. If something happens later that causes the buyer to leave negative feedback, you always have the opportunity to reply publicly to the buyer's accusations to go on record with your side of the story. You should *never* use feedback as a weapon, or "hijack" a buyer's feedback by threatening to leave negative feedback if a buyer is honest about her transaction with you.

chapter 13

Shipping Jewelry

Your final obligation as a seller after an auction closes is to ship the item to the buyer. If you haven't been paid, however, or your buyer's form of payment hasn't completely cleared yet, *you shouldn't even think about shipping the item.* I'll talk more about this in Chapter 14, "Protecting Yourself as a Seller," but remember that if the check is still in the mail, your item shouldn't be.

Let's assume, however, that you've been paid satisfactorily and that you're ready to pack up your jewelry or watch. Although many eBay sellers merely need to worry about having enough padded envelopes and bubble wrap on hand to pack up the items they've sold, sellers of jewelry and watches have many additional concerns. The jewelry industry suffers millions of dollars a year in thefts of shipped merchandise, carried out either as inside jobs by employees at courier companies or by thieves trolling neighborhoods and mailboxes to pilfer valuable-looking items. So, when shipping jewelry to your buyer, you need to be sure your jewelry is not only safe from the usual careless jostling, but also from sticky fingers.

Packing Materials

If you're planning to be a regular seller on eBay, you might want to go ahead and invest in a good supply of packaging material. Make a trip to your local discount store or office supply warehouse and stock up. When your item sells, you want to be prepared to quickly pack it up and send it off to your buyer, because speed is highly valued in the world of eBay transactions.

Here's what you'll need to get started:

- Hard-sided cardboard shipping boxes that are about the size of a shoebox or a 9-inch cube

- Smaller, flatter cardboard boxes (about 4 or 5 inches wide) with lids

- A few rolls or packages of bubble wrap

- Tissue paper

- Packaging tape

- Sticky labels

- If desired, pretty jewelry boxes or pouches in which to deliver your pieces—not necessary, but a nice, customer-oriented touch (you can buy empty boxes or pouches on eBay or wholesale on a number of Web sites)

You might also want to invest in a big box or container where you can keep all your materials. Otherwise, shipping materials tend to get scattered around the house. Also keep a good pair of scissors and a utility knife in your box so they'll always be handy when you need them.

Packing It Up

You'll now use the items you've purchased to pack jewelry in a way that not only keeps it from rattling around (and potentially breaking) during shipment, but also hides its true identity from thieves. Small, light boxes that make noise when you shake them are dead giveaways. Here's how to pack your jewelry so it remains anonymous:

1. Place a few layers of tissue paper in one of the smaller boxes, and then place your jewelry or watch on top of it. Place more layers of tissue paper on top of the jewelry, making sure to fill the gaps on the sides of the jewelry with the paper so the jewelry won't move around. Pack the box tightly with paper, and then tape the box closed.

2. Tape the smaller box to the inside of the larger box, and fill the remaining space with bubble wrap. This will protect the jewelry box, but it will also make the box feel heavier and therefore won't tip off thieves.

3. Place a packing slip inside the bigger box. This is a simple list of items that are included, which your recipient can use to check contents against what was shipped. In addition to an itemized list of contents, be sure to include a date, your name, and the recipient's name and address on the packing list. You might create this shipping list on your computer and print a copy for yourself as well, so you'll have a written record of what you shipped in case you need to file an insurance claim.

4. Tape the box closed using packing tape. After you've taped closed the opening, use extra tape to create a tougher layer, so thieves won't be able to snap the tape easily and quickly remove the contents.

Creating Your Label

Now, you're ready to create your label. Although it might seem less professional-looking, it's best to hand-write your label, because a typed label looks like it's being sent from a company and therefore suggests that the package contains valuable merchandise. Use a plain, white label with sticky backing, and write your return address and the recipient's name and address using the same format that you would if you were addressing an envelope, as shown in Figure 13.1.

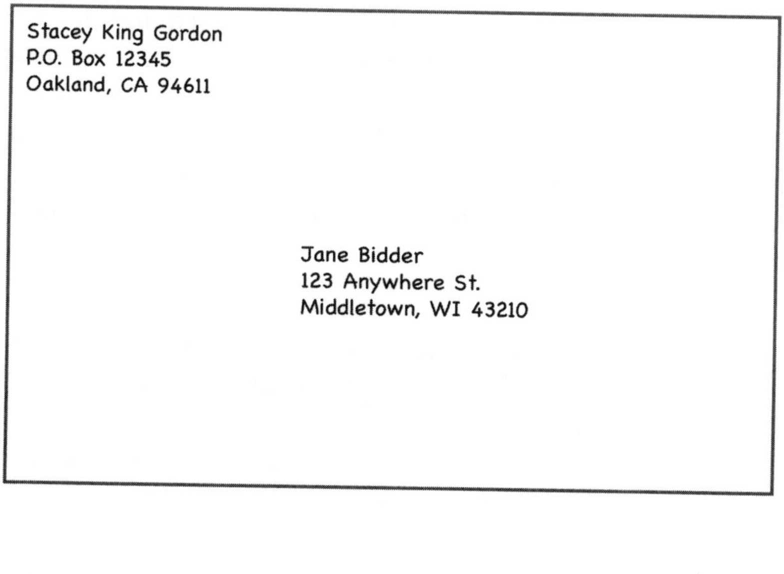

Stacey King Gordon
P.O. Box 12345
Oakland, CA 94611

Jane Bidder
123 Anywhere St.
Middletown, WI 43210

Figure 13.1

Hand-write your address label using a plain, white label. Write the return address, using initials for your company name, in the upper-left corner and your addressee's name in the middle of the label.

Most importantly, if you do business under a company name, *do not* use your company name in the return address, especially if the company name suggests that you are in the jewelry business. Instead, use initials for the name of your company, or simply use your personal name.

If you use a courier service that requires an airbill, make sure the document is firmly glued or stuck to the box. Some incidents have involved thieves who switch an original airbill with a new one that redirects the package to the wrong address.

Avoid writing "Handle with Care" or other indications that valuable items are enclosed. In fact, avoid writing on your package at all except for on your label. Experts say that anything you do to call attention to your package while it's sitting on the shipping dock can increase your risk of having your package tampered with or stolen. Also, if you are shipping outside of the country and are required to fill out a customs form, be sure to list the contents of the package as "parts" or "supplies," rather than the true description of your jewelry or watch.

Time to Ship

Now that your item is packed up, it's time to select a method of shipment. Security experts that specialize in the jewelry industry suggest a few wise strategies for keeping your shipment safe. Although you might instinctively feel more comfortable with a private courier service for your shipping, guess again. If you live in the United States, the U.S. Postal Service is actually the safest way to ship your item. The two major institutions specializing in security for the jewelry industry, Jewelers Security Alliance and Jewelers Mutual Insurance Company, recommend using U.S. first class registered mail whenever possible when shipping jewelry.

Why? Well, even though private couriers such as UPS and FedEx provide insurance for most kinds of jewelry items (UPS won't cover loose gemstones), the rate of theft is actually much higher with those services. With the exception of a couple of high-security shipping services that specialize in jewelry, which I'll discuss in a moment, the U.S. Postal Service has the best track record for keeping jewelry safe.

With U.S. first-class registered mail, items are placed under tight security from the time you turn them over to the postal employee until they arrive at your recipient's address. Items are insured up to $25,000. You'll be able to track the date and time of the delivery, as well as attempts at delivery, using the U.S. Postal Service's Web site, http://www.usps.gov, as shown in Figure 13.2. Fees for registered mail as of this writing start at $7.50 (on top of the regular postage for first class mail, which depends on the weight of your item), and increase depending on the insured value of the item.

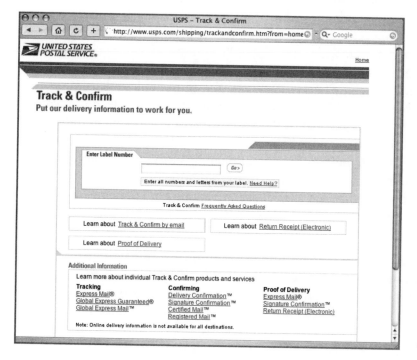

Figure 13.2

Use the U.S. Postal Service's Web site to track your packages and confirm that they're delivered.

First-class mail can take several days to be delivered. If you need the package to arrive sooner, the U.S. Postal Service's express mail service is your next-best option. Express mail ships to almost any address in the United States by the afternoon of the next day, and a signature is required for proof of delivery. Insurance is available up to $5,000. As of this writing, express mail rates start at $10.70 and increase depending on the weight of the item. Insurance starts at $1.30 for items valued at up to $50, and climbs incrementally from there.

Special Jewelry Delivery Services

If you are shipping very valuable items, from high-priced finished jewelry to loose gemstones to rare watches, you might not want to take a chance with ordinary shipping options. These special shipping services endorsed by the jewelry industry will almost literally guard your items with their lives:

■ **Parcel Pro Inc.** In 2003, Parcel Pro teamed up with Jewelers Mutual Insurance Company, the jewelry industry's premier insurance company, to offer insured, high-value shipping services to the industry. Parcel Pro provides next-day or second-day air service with up to $75,000 insurance (or more, upon request) for all domestic shipments, and next-day air with up to $30,000 insurance for international shipments. Each parcel is insured 100% at invoice value, and insurable items include loose gemstones. You must apply to become a member of Parcel Pro before you can use the service. To do so, you must first be a member of the Jewelers' Board of Trade (an industry organization that reviews the credit of retail jewelry operations and lists legitimate businesses in an annual directory) or of Polygon.net (an online community restricted to professionals in the jewelry industry). See Chapter 15, "Getting Serious About Selling," and visit http://www.parcelpro.com (see Figure 13.3) or call 1-888-683-2300 for more information about becoming a member of these organizations.

■ **Brinks.** When you think Brinks, you probably think armored vehicles. But Brinks also offers highly secure shipping for diamonds and jewelry through its Brinks Diamond and Jewelry Services. Brinks is known the world over for transporting some of the most valuable goods transacted in history. The company will insure your item for its total value, takes total responsibility if the item is lost or stolen, and will often fill claims within 72 hours. Keep in mind that this shipping option is probably realistic only if you're selling something that's truly priceless—very expensive and virtually irreplaceable. Nonetheless, it's reassuring to know that the service exists if you ever should need it. Visit http://www.brinksdjs.com or call 1-800-267-1289 for more information.

Figure 13.3

Parcel Pro is one of the insured shipping services available to jewelry sellers.

A Few Shipping Precautions

Before you ship, follow these tried and true strategies to keep your package extra safe.

- **Never ship over a weekend.** Don't time your shipment so that the package will need to sit in a distribution center over a weekend. That dead time gives thieves a couple extra days to lift your valuable.

- **Track your package.** Be sure to get a tracking number and check the status of your item from time to time. All courier services (including the U.S. Postal Service if you use registered mail, express mail, or priority mail) offer shipment tracking on their Web sites.

- **Get a signature.** You want to make your delivery as convenient as possible, but you also want to make sure your package stays safe. So let your buyer know that you will ship the item with a signature required, so the courier can't simply leave the box on the doorstep if nobody's home. If necessary, the recipient will need to go to the post office or courier pick-up location in person to retrieve the package. It's a pain, but it's better than a criminal retrieving the package instead.

■ **Take care with certain ZIP codes.** Expert thieves know that a higher percentage of jewelry and gemstones is shipped to and from a handful of ZIP codes: 10036 (New York City); 90013, 90014, and 90015 (Los Angeles); 60602, 60603, and 60659 (Chicago); and 94102, 94103, and 94108 (San Francisco). These are ZIP codes that include major jewelry centers or many jewelry businesses. Take extra precautions to disguise and track your package if shipping to any of these areas.

chapter 14

Protecting Yourself
as a Seller

You want to begin your life as an eBay seller believing wholeheartedly in the honesty of the eBay community members. But at the same time, you have to keep your eyes open. The risks you run as an eBay seller are the same as any merchant in the offline world. There's always the possibility of "shoplifting"—a shopper taking your merchandise without paying for it. But you also have the murkier problems of fraud, having to do with stolen credit cards, identity theft, and other modern-day scams.

For the most part, contending with these risks involves keeping your eyes open and using common sense. Fortunately, however, eBay also offers some formal protection programs to help shield you from dishonest community members. This chapter looks at a few common schemes and other problems, and offers you guidelines on how to deal with each one.

Nonpaying Bidders

The problem of eBay members who bid, win, and don't pay is the most common issue eBay sellers will face. Although most bidders mean well, every once in awhile you'll encounter an eBay member who is new to the site and doesn't really understand the rules. If the mood strikes, they'll bid on your item, but winning the auction might take them by surprise. Suffering a healthy dose of buyers' remorse, they might slink off and never respond to your requests for payment.

How do you deal with these nonpaying bidders? First, give the winning bidder the benefit of the doubt. Life happens, circumstances change, things come up. Your bidder might suddenly have been called out of town, or might be dealing with a family emergency or an unexpected work obligation, and might forget all about her late-night impulsive bid on your eBay item. So after you send your invoice to her, wait a few days, and then e-mail her again. In fact, you might send her two or three e-mails before you start to suspect something's wrong. Don't immediately assume your bidder has skipped town. But by the third e-mail, you should be clear about how you plan to proceed if you don't hear from her. Your options include the following:

- Telephoning the buyer
- Reporting the buyer to eBay by filing an Unpaid Item dispute

And of course, you always have the option of relisting the auction within a certain period of time.

Telephoning the Buyer

If after your attempts at gentle prodding via e-mail you still don't hear from your buyer, you can request her contact information from eBay and call her. See Chapter 8, "The Good, the Bad, and the Ugly," for instructions on requesting contact information. When you request the buyer's contact information, an e-mail will be sent to the buyer with your own contact information, so she has the chance to get in touch with you, too.

Do attempt to get in touch with your bidder by phone before taking any action against the buyer—it's the habit of a good, service-oriented seller. Often in these situations you'll hear the voice of a very embarrassed buyer who has been meaning to get around to sending payment but has been too busy. All will be well, and you'll probably earn great feedback and a loyal customer out of the transaction, as opposed to closing the deal on a sour note.

On the other hand, maybe you won't get in touch with the bidder. She might not answer her phone or return your calls if you leave messages. You might reach a recording informing you that the phone number has been disconnected or is no longer in service. After a couple of days of getting signs like this, it's probably safe to assume that you'll never hear from this bidder again.

Filing an Unpaid Item Dispute

Seven days after the listing ends, if you have not yet received payment from your buyer, you are entitled to file an Unpaid Item dispute. The benefits of doing so—rather than simply forgetting the situation and moving on—are twofold:

- You will help send a clear message to the user that she can't continue to behave badly on eBay, a moral obligation you have as an upstanding community member. If a user racks up three Unpaid Item disputes, she'll be automatically suspended from the site—so you're helping to protect other sellers against this careless bidder.

- eBay will refund your final value fee, plus permit you to relist your item free of charge. (Simply you use the Relist option as outlined in Chapter 12, "Sealing the Deal," and your listing fee will be waived.)

Here's how to file a dispute:

1. Go to http://pages.ebay.com/help/policies/unpaid-item.html.

2. Click File an Unpaid Item dispute.

3. In the pop-up window, enter the item number of the auction that the bidder won. Click Continue.

4. On the page shown in Figure 14.1, select Buyer has not paid for the item from the first pull-down menu. From the second pull-down menu, select the situation that best applies to you (such as "The buyer has not responded"). Click Continue.

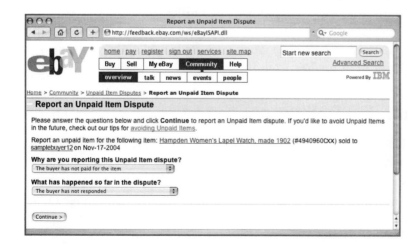

Figure 14.1

When you enter your item number, eBay will automatically find the winning bidder's name and ask you for the reason you're filing the Unpaid Item dispute.

5. On the next screen, click Send an Unpaid Item Reminder. An e-mail will be sent to the bidder from eBay reminding her to pay for the item she won. This e-mail will provide the bidder with a number of options to respond to you, including paying immediately for the item to close the dispute.

6. Under the Related Links menu in My eBay, click Unpaid Item Disputes to monitor the status of the claim.

7. Eventually, you'll either resolve the dispute or give up hope and claim your reimbursement. To close your dispute, click Related Links in My eBay, click Unpaid Item Disputes, and select an option based on your situation:

   ■ If the buyer responds at least once after she receives the notice from eBay and you both work out a satisfactory payment arrangement, you can select the option notifying eBay that you and the buyer have completed the transaction satisfactorily, in which case the bidder does not receive an Unpaid Item strike and you do not receive a credit for your final value fee.

   ■ If you and the bidder have mutually agreed not to complete the transaction, you can select an option notifying eBay of that fact, which means the buyer does not receive an Unpaid Item strike, but you get a credit for your final value fee. (And you get to relist your item for free.)

   ■ If the buyer does not respond within seven days, you can select the option notifying eBay that you no longer wish to attempt communication with the bidder. The bidder receives an Unpaid Item strike, and you receive a credit in the amount of the final value fee you were charged when your item sold. (And you get to relist your item for free.)

No Dough, No Delivery

This is the golden rule of selling on eBay. As I mentioned in Chapter 13, "Shipping Jewelry," no matter what kinds of elaborate stories you hear, no matter how sweet your bidder seems to be, you should in no circumstances ship an item until you receive a payment and have verified that the payment is legitimate. If that means waiting several days for a check to clear, just be patient. This is the safest way to ensure you will get the money you're owed.

Unhappy Buyers

After you've shipped the item, you might think you've washed your hands of the transaction. But then you log in to your e-mail one morning to find an angry e-mail from your buyer, who insists he never received your package, or that it arrived irreparably damaged. Or maybe he is accusing you of misrepresenting the item, demanding that the jewelry he received looks nothing like the jewelry in your photo. Worse, the buyer might have bypassed e-mail communication altogether and gone straight for the jugular: your Feedback rating.

You're immediately enraged, and you're ready to seek vengeance. How dare this person accuse you of being less than honest? But before you fly off the handle and do something destructive, take a few deep breaths. Then address the situation the way a mature, honest, upstanding eBayer would.

Getting to the Bottom of It

Your first step is to request your buyer's contact information and give him a call. Sometimes a phone call is all it takes to cool tempers, and a buyer is less likely to be stubborn and nasty if you're speaking to him personally. It's so easy to create misunderstandings through e-mail, especially in tone, so a polite, reasonable conversation is often the only thing that's necessary. Keep your cool during the call and remain professional and courteous—remember, this is your customer, and, in theory at least, the customer is always right.

What's the purpose of the call? You want to let the buyer know you're concerned about the situation, but you also want to get more details. Most people aren't good at expressing themselves in writing, so the buyer might have left out important details in his complaint. It's also a good way for you to ask some questions that the buyer might not have thought to ask, and to tell your side of the story. "I packed the item in several layers of bubble wrap and double-boxed the shipment to you, so I'm really surprised to hear that the item was damaged. I plan to file an insurance claim with my shipper, so I'd appreciate any details you could give me about the damage." Or: "I think it's strange that you never received the item. When I look up the tracking number, my shipper is showing the package was delivered. Is it possible a neighbor picked it up for you, or that it's behind your bushes or at a side or back porch?"

Although you should express concern, approach the situation as you would a car accident. Unless you realize right away within the first few minutes of the conversation that you are undoubtedly at fault and you plan to reimburse your buyer, *do not* admit that you are at fault outright. To protect yourself, stay neutral until you understand what really happened. If you and the buyer must go through a formal dispute resolution process later, you won't want to be in the situation of having apologized or admitted you were to blame.

Resolving the Situation

You and your buyer can talk about how to handle the situation to make sure you both are satisfied with the outcome. Here are some recommendations on how to handle different situations:

- **The buyer doesn't like the item.** If the issue is simply that the buyer is not happy with the item or doesn't feel you accurately represented what you sold to him, the fair thing to do is to offer a full refund. Of course, as a seller, you can determine how long after the end of the auction you'll extend this refund. You also want to be sure to only give the buyer his money back if he has returned the item to you in the same condition in which you shipped it.

- **The buyer claims the item is damaged.** If the issue involves a supposedly damaged item, ask the buyer to take a picture of the item and e-mail it to you for insurance purposes. From this photo, you can determine whether the claim is legitimate, and then use it to submit an insurance claim to the U.S. Postal Service or shipping company. You might make a habit of taking pictures of the item as you package it—some sellers even videotape themselves packing up the item—to prove the item was in fine condition before you shipped it. Be sure to turn on your time and date stamp function in your camera to prove you took the picture immediately before you shipped the item.

- **The buyer claims the item never arrived.** If you used registered mail, priority mail, or any private courier service, you will be able to track a package. If the package is delivered successfully, your tracking number will allow you to see exactly when it was delivered and, in some cases, who signed for it. If you can't verify that the package ever arrived, or you suspect it didn't, you can file an insurance claim through your shipper. Stay in close communication with the buyer to let him know that you'll reimburse him as soon the shipper reimburses you.

Using Mediation

If you just can't work out the situation on your own, don't let the deal end badly. You can get some help from eBay and the mediation company it endorses, SquareTrade. This online dispute resolution services, located at http://www.squaretrade.com, will work with both you and the buyer to reach a fair compromise. SquareTrade works in two phases:

1. First, you file a claim through SquareTrade, telling your side of the story (see Figure 14.2). SquareTrade then contacts the buyer, who has an opportunity to submit his version of what happened. Then the two of you can attempt to work things out on your own using Direct Negotiation, SquareTrade's Web-based communications tool. This service is free.

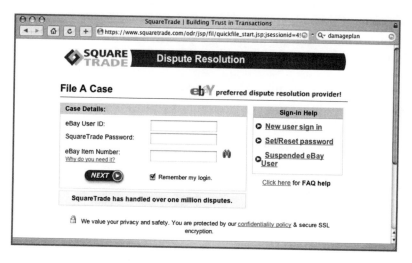

Figure 14.2

Use SquareTrade's communications tool as a neutral place where you can work out your differences with your buyer.

2. If Direct Negotiation doesn't work, a SquareTrade professional mediator can step in to guide the process. This service requires a fee. The mediator does not act as a judge, but instead facilitates solution-oriented resolution. The mediator *will* make a recommendation for resolution only if both parties request it.

Handling Negative Feedback

If a dispute with a buyer has resulted in one or both of you dealing the blow of negative feedback, you can negotiate with the buyer to mutually withdraw that feedback. Both the buyer and the seller must undergo the feedback-removal process for the feedback to be withdrawn; after reviewing the feedback-removal request, eBay removes the feedback on your behalf. Alternatively, if SquareTrade or another dispute-resolution service delivers a ruling or settlement to eBay at the end of a dispute, eBay will remove the feedback.

If you and your buyer agree to remove negative feedback, you both must do the following:

1. Go to http://pages.ebay.com/help/policies/feedback-removal.html.

2. Click Mutual Feedback Withdrawal.

3. Enter the item number of the disputed auction, and click Continue.

4. Review the auction information and the feedback that both you and the buyer left. If desired, enter a short message to the buyer—a note explaining why she's receiving this message. Then click Continue. The request will be sent to eBay and to the buyer.

The important thing to remember is that if something negative happens with a buyer, you shouldn't throw up your hands and walk away. Doing so will make you gun-shy and suspicious of every bidder going forward. If you dig a little deeper, you will probably find there's more going on than what you see on the surface. Make an attempt, whenever possible, to resolve the situation so both parties are satisfied. In other words, be the bigger eBayer.

Fraud on eBay

You are more likely to run into situations like the ones I described in the preceding sections than to encounter scams or fraudulent activity on eBay. Nevertheless, like all other channels online and offline, eBay does have its share of charlatans looking to pull a fast one on gullible eBay members. The trick is to *not* be one of the naïve ones.

Although the details of fraudulent activity vary widely and colorfully from scheme to scheme, most types that sellers will encounter fall into two broad categories:

- **Misrepresentation of identity.** This may include use of a stolen credit card (which can hurt a seller, because the credit-card company will most likely reclaim the money when they discover the theft) or a hijacked eBay account (which involves a thief who uses an eBay community member's user ID to bid on and pay for items, diverting the shipment of the item to another address for the thief to claim). More common for buyers, but also a danger for sellers, are e-mails disguised as communications from eBay, instructing you to click a link to log in to your account right away to deal with some alarming or urgent issue. When you click on the link, you're directed to a site on another server that *looks* like eBay, but isn't. There, you are usually asked to enter personal and financial information, which is then whisked away into these crooks' computers and used for ill-gotten gain.

- **Blatant scams.** You receive an e-mail from your bidder in Russia or Romania, begging you to ship your diamond necklace in time for a big wedding party that's coming up. The eBayer promises to transfer money into an escrow account for you to pick up, but when you go to fetch the money, you realize the escrow account is bogus. There are hundreds of scenarios like this—find a whole discussion board about the various proliferations of them by clicking Community, then Discussion Boards, then Trust & Safety (Safe Harbor).

The important thing to remember is to never ship an item unless you have the payment in hand, however persuasively your buyer begs you to do otherwise. Also, only ship to a *verified billing address*, which is the address used on the buyer's PayPal or credit-card account. (It's harder to determine this address with money orders and checks, which is why PayPal is preferable.)

Most crucially, trust your instincts if you think something might be fishy. Do a little investigating into a situation before automatically shipping the item.

Reporting a Scam

If you receive an e-mail that appears to be spam disguised as eBay e-mail, or if something is obviously fishy with a buyer's account or payment, you should contact eBay right away. eBay operates a fraud-prevention division called Safe Harbor that collects these cases, hunts down the perpetrators, and tries to make sure they are booted off eBay. To report suspicious activity, do the following:

1. Go to http://pages.ebay.com/securitycenter.

2. Select the option button beside the problem you wish to report. As shown in Figure 14.3, you have three options: Spoof (fake) email, Unpaid item, or Report another problem. In this example, I've clicked the Report another problem option button.

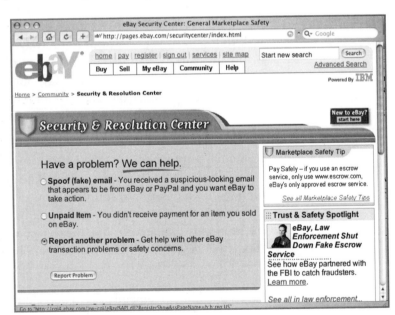

Figure 14.3

Use eBay's Security Center to report scams, spoofs, and other suspicious activity.

3. On the next page, select from the first list of statements about the nature of your problem. A sublist will appear in the second box; its contents depend on what you select in the first box. Yet another sublist will appear in the third box based on your second selection, as shown in Figure 14.4. When you've made your selections, click Continue.

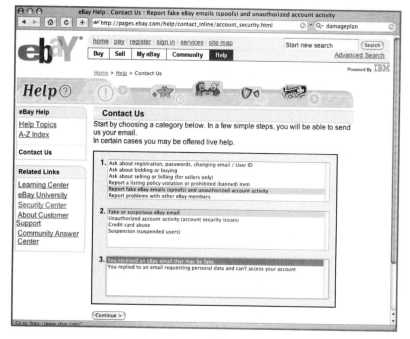

Figure 14.4

Use eBay's preformulated reason lists to best sum up your own situation and reason for filing a report.

4. The next page will direct you to either read more on the subject or contact eBay directly via e-mail. Click Email to continue with your report.

5. Depending on your issue, the next page will feature the appropriate report form. For example, as shown in Figure 14.5, if you're reporting a spoof e-mail, the form will include fields where you can paste the text that was in the e-mail you received.

After you file your form, eBay will notify you in a day or two that your report was received, and that eBay is investigating the matter.

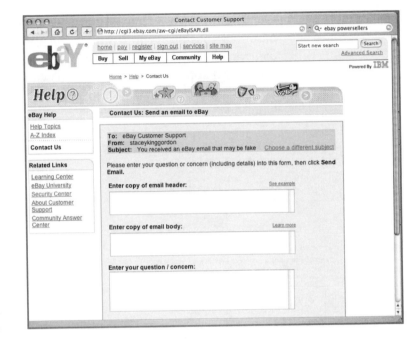

Figure 14.5

The appropriate report form will appear to allow you to submit full details about the concern you're reporting.

PayPal's Seller Protection Policy

eBay *does not* cover sellers under its Fraud Alert and Protection Claim program. It strongly cautions sellers, as I have here, to only ship items after payment is received and leaves it at that. But what if you *have* received payment, only to find that the charges are reversed later due to fraud? *Chargebacks* happen when a person reports unauthorized use of her credit card or PayPal account. Typically when this occurs, the credit-card company will stop payment or reclaim the funds already paid out. Or, if the buyer claim is submitted through PayPal, PayPal will place a temporary hold on the money, which means a seller can't claim it and cash it in. This obviously isn't fair to the seller; it's too bad the buyer had her identify and information stolen, but it isn't *your* fault. And yet, your valuable item might very well be on its way to wherever you shipped it, and you are—at least temporarily—out of luck.

The good news is that, if you accept PayPal and the transaction that resulted in the chargeback was a PayPal payment, you are backed by special protection.

PayPal's Seller Protection Policy offers insurance of up to $5,000 to sellers who receive chargebacks due to fraud—for example, if the seller has sold to a buyer who used a credit card illegally, hijacked an account, or otherwise got out of rightfully paying for the item. However, to be eligible for this insurance, you must follow PayPal's recipe for "low-risk" transactions. You can only take advantage of this coverage if you

- Have a verified Business or Premier account on PayPal.

- Ship within seven days after the auction is over, and keep your shipping document to show you shipped to the correct address.

- Require a signature receipt for items worth more than $250.

- Accept your entire payment in a single transaction with the buyer.

- Respond to all PayPal inquiries in a timely manner.

- Have shipped to a buyer who lives in one of the 45 countries "approved" by PayPal (see Table 14.1 for a list of these countries). PayPal does not provide service in countries where there is a high rate of fraud.

Table 14.1 PayPal-Approved Countries

Anguilla	Argentina	Australia
Austria	Belgium	Brazil
Canada	Chile	China
Costa Rica	Denmark	Dominican Republic
Ecuador	Finland	France
Germany	Greece	Hong Kong
Iceland	India	Ireland
Israel	Italy	Jamaica
Japan	Luxembourg	Malaysia
Mexico	Monaco	Netherlands
New Zealand	Norway	Portugal
Singapore	South Korea	Spain
Sweden	Switzerland	Taiwan
Thailand	Turkey	United Kingdom
United States	Uruguay	Venezuela

That's why PayPal offers this protection program. If you are a PayPal member and a chargeback is placed on one of your transactions, contact PayPal right away. To report the problem, do the following:

1. Go to http://www.paypal.com and click Security Center on the bottom menu.

2. Under For Sellers, click Report a Problem.

3. Select Protections/Privacy/Security from the left menu, then select Seller Protection Policy from the right menu, as shown in Figure 14.6.

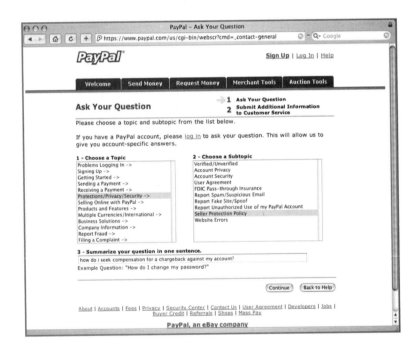

Figure 14.6

Select topics related to seller protection when going through the process of reporting your problem.

4. In the Summarize your question in one sentence field, type something along the lines of **How do I seek compensation for a chargeback against my account?** Click Continue.

5. In the Additional Information form, provide details about your case. You have up to 1,000 characters to explain your situation. Click Continue to submit your inquiry instantly.

chapter 15

Getting Serious About Selling

As you begin to get a taste for selling jewelry and watches on eBay, the possibilities might suddenly start to seem endless—and overwhelming. At the same time that you're getting ideas for your new business—ways to promote yourself, sources for your merchandise, new techniques for photographing items and writing descriptions—you're also gradually beginning to understand just how much time the process takes. You might also discover quickly how much you have left to learn, both about eBay and about jewelry.

These realizations are growing pains; they're simply signs that you're ready to move on to the next level of eBay selling. This chapter covers some essential next steps if you're *serious* about getting serious as an eBay seller.

Serious About eBay

So you've decided that eBay really is for you. As a seller of jewelry and watches, whether you're a professional, a hobbyist, or an amateur, you like the potential for profit that the world's largest online marketplace offers. Furthermore, you enjoy the pure thrill of selling something so precious and beautiful to such eager customers.

Before you decide to devote yourself full tilt to the eBay seller's life, you'll need to expand both your capabilities and offerings so you can stay competitive in this cutthroat marketplace. You'll also need a little help—so you'll stay sane. This section delves into some of the basics of setting yourself apart and better managing your time and resources.

Becoming a PowerSeller

As you grow into a professional eBay seller, you should keep you eye on one ball in particular: becoming a PowerSeller. This is an honorable distinction that will set you apart from many other sellers. As a PowerSeller, you're in an exclusive group. Yet it seems like everybody who uses eBay recognizes the, er, *power* of the PowerSeller label, which communicates to bidders that you are reputable, honest, and knowledgeable.

To become a PowerSeller, you must achieve $1,000 in sales each month for three continuous months. You also must

- Have at least 100 unique feedback results, 98 percent of which are positive.

- Have on average a total of four listings per month for the past three months.

- Comply with eBay listing policies.

- Contact bidders within three business days and keep your account current.

Once you've achieved that milestone, eBay will automatically e-mail you to invite you to become a PowerSeller. The privilege of becoming a PowerSeller is free, and also offers perks such as dedicated customer service, a special portal and forum, a tool for easily creating banner ads, and more.

Tip

If you've reached your $1,000 milestone and haven't received an invitation to become a PowerSeller, check your eBay Preferences to make sure you're allowing eBay to contact you by e-mail. Simply go to My eBay and click eBay Preferences on the left menu. Then, as shown in Figure 15.1, click view/change next to Notification preferences, and check the box next to eBay Email.

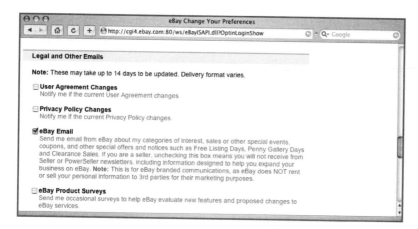

Figure 15.1

Use your eBay Preferences to ensure you can receive e-mail notifications from eBay when you become eligible to be a PowerSeller.

After you've attained the PowerSeller sales requirement, you have the opportunity to climb to five different tiers:

1. **Bronze:** $1,000 in sales each month
2. **Silver:** $3,000 in sales each month
3. **Gold:** $10,000 in sales each month
4. **Platinum:** $25,000 in sales each month
5. **Titanium:** $150,000 in sales each month

With the achievement of each new tier, you'll earn an extra set of benefits. For example, platinum and titanium PowerSellers earn support by dedicated account managers.

Resources for Auction Management

When you're just offering one or two auctions, the usual method of listing, watching, managing, and closing an auction—using eBay's simple forms and monitoring your activity from My eBay—is probably good enough. But down the road, when you get the hang of selling on eBay and think you might like to get serious about it, you're going to need some help. Listing items can take 15 or 20 minutes apiece, and when you're selling dozens of items, who has that kind of time? Plus, watching your bidders, managing communications, and invoicing auction winners are all obligations that require time and attention to detail.

At this point, it might be helpful to consider getting some help—namely, automatic auction listing and management tools. eBay itself offers many of these tools, as do a number of other companies. This section outlines some of your options.

Listing Managers

These listing-management tools enable you to bulk-list your items, create more professional-looking listings, and automatically relist your items if they don't sell.

- **eBay Turbo Lister (http://pages.ebay.com/turbo_lister).** This free online tool, shown in Figure 15.2, allows you to list and edit all your auctions from a single page, plus schedule your listing times and import current or past items into your new listing.

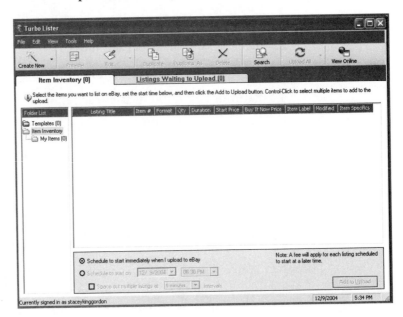

Figure 15.2

eBay Turbo Lister is a free, easy way to bulk-list many items at once, and edit them after you've posted them.

- **eBay Seller Manager (http://pages.ebay.com/selling_manager/products.html).** Seller Manager and Seller Manager Pro are Web-based tools that enable you to bulk-list, track all your listings from a single spot, manage e-mails with buyers, and with Seller Manager Pro, download monthly reports and manage non-paying bidders. Seller Manager is $4.99 a month; Seller Manager Pro is $9.99 a month.

■ **eBay Seller's Assistant (http://pages.ebay.com/sellers_assistant).**
You can install this software program on your PC's hard drive and
use it to create and edit all your listings without being connected to
the Internet. Then you can easily manage all your auctions from one
spot, effortlessly invoice buyers and print shipping labels, and even
print profitability and sales reports. The software, shown in Figure 15.3,
comes in a regular ($9.99 a month) and Pro ($24.99 a month) version.

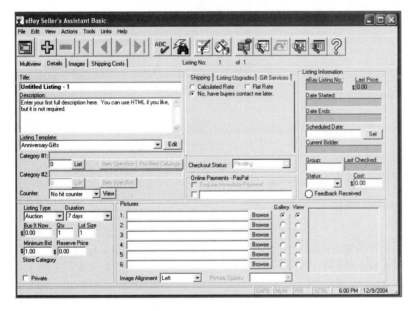

Figure 15.3

Seller's Assistant allows
you to work offline, and then
upload your auctions to eBay
at one time.

■ **Andale Auction Lister (http://www.andale.com/sell/sell_quickstart.jsp).**
Also available in a regular and Pro version, this tool provides many
of the same capabilities as eBay Seller's Assistant but with a few more
sophisticated features. Some of the exceptional capabilities include a
design center with more than 100 layout choices, selling recommendations based on research involving pricing and success rates, and
an automatic "price compare" function in your eBay listing to show
buyers how your Buy It Now price compares with similar past items.
Prices are based on the number of listings you post each month,
starting at $2 for 10 listings.

■ **Auctiva Poster (http://www.auctiva.com/products/AuctivaPoster.aspx).**
Also a bulk lister, as shown in Figure 15.4, this tool provides capabilities
for multiple auction and e-commerce sites—which means you can
use it to branch out from eBay into Amazon Auctions, Amazon zShops,
and Yahoo!. You can store preferences and automatically pre-fill many
of your fields every time you list an auction, saving valuable time.
The professional version, Auctiva Poster, is $9.95 a month; there's
also a free version, Mr. Poster, with fewer features.

Figure 15.4

Auctiva offers a listing tool that
works with eBay and other
auction services, in case
you're ready to branch
out to sites beyond eBay.

There are easily a few dozen other services that offer auction listing services.
Some are free and basic, and others offer the same kinds of services that the
tools listed here provide. The Web site Auction Insights keeps a complete list
of these tools at http://www.auctioninsights.com/selling-on-ebay.html.

Other Tools

Although the paid auction listing programs I previously mentioned give you
pretty complete packages of tools, you can also seek out unbundled services
that address your specific needs. Here are a few examples:

- **Research.** Andale offers individual tools for research-specific aspects of building your selling business. Tools help you research the right price at which to start and sell your product, provide a database of sellers who can help you source your merchandise, and provide a summary of what the hot sellers are in your category.

- **Counters and trackers.** As with any Web site, you want to find out how many people are looking at your page and, if you're really serious, how they found you. There are dozens of options available for tracking your auction hits. Some of them you can make visible on your site for the world to see, while others provide detailed statistical information. Free counters are available from Andale (http://www.andale.com), Shoporium (http://www.shoporium.com/counters), and Amherst Robots (http://www.vrane.com). One cool option is ViewTracker, a free program that lets you see what keywords and categories buyers used to find your listing (http://www.sellathon.com). See an example in Figure 15.5.

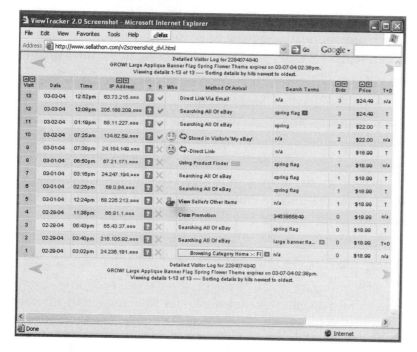

Figure 15.5

ViewTracker gives you insight into how people are searching for, and finding, your auction listings.

Setting Up Your eBay Store

The sign that you're on eBay to stay is when you look into setting up your eBay store. An eBay store is a single place to consolidate all your items for sale. It also allows you to sell items at fixed retail prices instead of only listing auctions. Similar to other user-friendly e-commerce shops such as Yahoo! and Amazon zShops, eBay provides an easy format for getting an e-business up and running, and it helps you establish credibility with buyers, proving that you're a legitimate merchant.

If you're trying to establish a business and build an online brand, eBay stores offer a viable option for you. Starting at $9.95 a month (plus fees when your items sell and other optional upgrade fees), the service offers you the option of posting auctions for up to 120 days or even indefinitely. You also get a cross-promotion tool, a site design that you can customize, your own domain name, and a search engine.

The idea behind opening an eBay store is to build repeat business, open your eBay business up to people who don't necessarily like the auction format, and offer additional promotional resources to encourage sales. According to eBay, on average, sellers see a 25 percent increase in sales in the three months following the opening of their eBay stores.

On the other hand, some sellers have said they don't see enough traffic to their stores to warrant the extra fees. Visitors to eBay typically are unaware of the stores and might only click through to them if they are interested in buying more from a specific seller. In the study by the Jewelry Consumer Opinion Council of jewelry buyers who used eBay, which I discussed in Chapter 10, "eBay for the Jewelry Professional," around 57 percent of eBay jewelry shoppers said they do not buy from eBay stores, while another 20 percent said they weren't sure. This lack of awareness among many eBay buyers means that, unless there's a clear cross-promotion linking auctions to stores, buyers might never wander over to the other side of the fence.

So how do you know if opening an eBay store is for you? You might seriously consider setting up a store for your business if

■ **You want to establish a theme.** You have moved beyond selling any piece of jewelry you can get your hands on. You've established reliable sources and a strong knowledge base, and you want to create a niche business selling only vintage chandelier earrings, loose South American–mined gemstones, or other related items. Opening an eBay store is a great way to get your name out there. Such a focused business can put you in front of buyers who perform keyword searches for hot niche items.

- **You attract repeat customers.** If you've begun to notice that the jewelry you sell is developing a small following with buyers who return to search your auctions again and again, an eBay store lets you set up a Mecca for your devoted buyers.

- **You offer a mix of auctions and fixed-price sales.** Often, sellers attract buyers to their stores through their auctions. If buyers like what they see, they'll return to look for the new items that sellers post for fixed prices. To treat an eBay store as solely an online retail shop is probably not the best use of the tool; eBay stores offer you the chance to cross-promote your auctions with your other sales.

- **You're willing to put time into marketing.** With the price of your eBay store, you get a complimentary cross-promotion tool, allowing you to easily promote your other items in each listing, as well as an e-mail marketing tool that allows you to create custom-designed e-mail newsletters. As with any business, you need to invest time in marketing to drive traffic to your site—enough has been discovered about the Internet, and retail in general, to understand that if you build it, they won't necessarily come. The harder you work to promote your store, the more successful you will be.

How to Register for a Store

eBay makes it especially enticing to sign up for an eBay store by giving you the first 30 days free. To sign up, do the following:

1. Got to http://pages.ebay.com/stores.

2. Click Open a Store Now!

3. Click I Accept the eBay User Agreement.

4. Choose the theme (color and design) of your store by selecting the option button beside the template you want. Click Continue.

5. As shown in Figure 15.6, you can enter the name and write a short description of your store that will show up when buyers browse the main eBay Stores page.

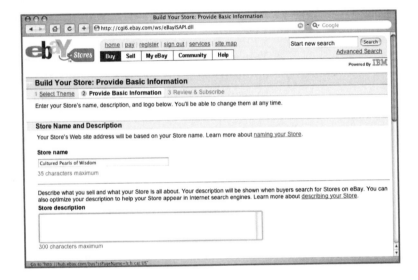

Figure 15.6

Customize your store by entering your business name and writing an enticing description to attract buyers to your store.

6. Select a store logo, as shown in Figure 15.7. Choose a predesigned logo (for example, an icon of a ring or gemstone), or upload your own graphic to use as a logo. Alternatively, you can select the option button beside Do not display a logo. Click Continue.

7. Select the option button beside the service to which you want to subscribe. Choose from Basic ($9.95 a month), Featured ($49.95 a month), or Anchor ($499.95). A basic store is a good place to start if you just want to try out the eBay Stores format; a featured store is a logical upgrade once you begin to get the hang of it, because you'll get sales reports, inventory management tools, and other merchant resources. Then click Start My Subscription Now.

You're up and running now! eBay will automatically add any of your existing auction listings to your store. You can continue to customize your store by clicking Continue Customizing, which will allow you to set preferences about how your information is displayed.

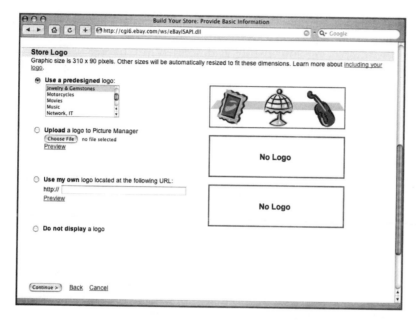

Figure 15.7

Select from a series of options for artwork you can use as your store logo.

Listing Items in Your Store

Anytime you list an auction or a fixed-price item, it will automatically appear in your store. You also have the option of listing items *only* in your store, which provides the benefit of lower listing fees and longer listing durations —but it prevents your items from showing up in search-engine results outside of your store.

To list your item as part of your store, do the following:

1. Click the Sell tab.

2. Select one of three options:

   ■ **Sell Item at Online Auction.** Your item will be listed in auction format, where buyers can bid to win the item.

   ■ **Sell Item at Fixed Price.** Your item will be listed as Buy It Now only.

   ■ **Sell in Store Inventory.** Your item will be listed as Buy It Now only, and will appear only in your eBay Store.

3. Click Continue

4. Proceed with creating your listing as described in Chapter 9, "From Buyer to Seller."

Serious About Jewelry

Now that you've found ways to sell with success on eBay, you might consider becoming an established member of the jewelry industry, if you aren't already. For all the reasons I've repeated throughout this book, becoming a more educated, professional merchant of jewelry is crucial to your future success. You want to be an expert not only to protect yourself, but also to simply compete—especially on eBay, where many of your fellow sellers are already certified industry members. While you're certainly not expected to get a degree in gemology or open up a retail storefront anytime soon, you might consider some of the options in this section if you're serious about selling jewelry and watches.

Industry Membership

In the world of online jewelry, there are two very important distinctions without which you won't get very far: a Jewelers Board of Trade number and a Polygon ID. These two affiliations have become standards in the jewelry industry, and they can open a lot of doors for you. For example, you might need them to have access to:

- Business relationships with many established wholesalers, manufacturers, exporters, and drop-ship suppliers
- Admittance to industry trade shows and wholesale jewelry marts
- Membership in prestigious online communities
- Certain insurance and shipping services (including Brinks)

Before you read on, keep in mind that you need to be a serious seller—that is, an established merchant with a business license and a resale tax ID number—before you venture into this territory. The jewelry industry is rightfully protective, for security and competitive reasons, and the people with whom you're dealing will use these two distinctions as a signal that they can take you seriously.

Jewelers Board of Trade

The Jewelers Board of Trade (JBT) is a non-profit organization that lists jewelry retailers and maintains credit information on them. Manufacturers and wholesalers that are members of JBT receive the JBT *Red Book*, which lists all retailers and their credit rating. These companies base their decisions on whether or not to do business with the listed retailers based on their credit rating. Needless to say, your JBT rating can make or break your jewelry business.

It's free to get a JBT listing, and with your listing you receive a number. Because JBT prescreens a business and essentially gets to the bottom of that business's practices, the JBT number has become a standard for determining whether a company is a legitimate part of the industry. From time to time, as you become more established, you'll see a request for your Jewelers Board of Trade number.

Keep in mind that a Jewelers Board of Trade listing is not for everybody. You must be a true retail company, even if your primary channel is the Internet. You'll be asked for your resale tax ID number, all your financials, and other information about your business. If you're a casual seller only, there's no need to bother applying for a number. But if you have established your business, created a company name, and have been selling full-time (or even part-time but are doing big business) for a while, consider getting a free JBT listing. To do so, visit http://www.jewelersboard.com/contact, shown in Figure 15.8, and click Download and print a listing form now to download a PDF application form.

Polygon.net

When the Internet began permeating the jewelry industry, Polygon.net became the first truly influential online network for industry members. It established security standards for industry Web sites (namely, the TradeLock password, which now protects industry-only sections of many jewelry organization sites) and allowed jewelers to easily build their own Web sites. More importantly, it established a Web-based trading channel for suppliers and retailers, including CertNet, a diamond database, which allows jewelers to quickly and securely search for diamonds in wholesalers' inventories to meet customers' needs.

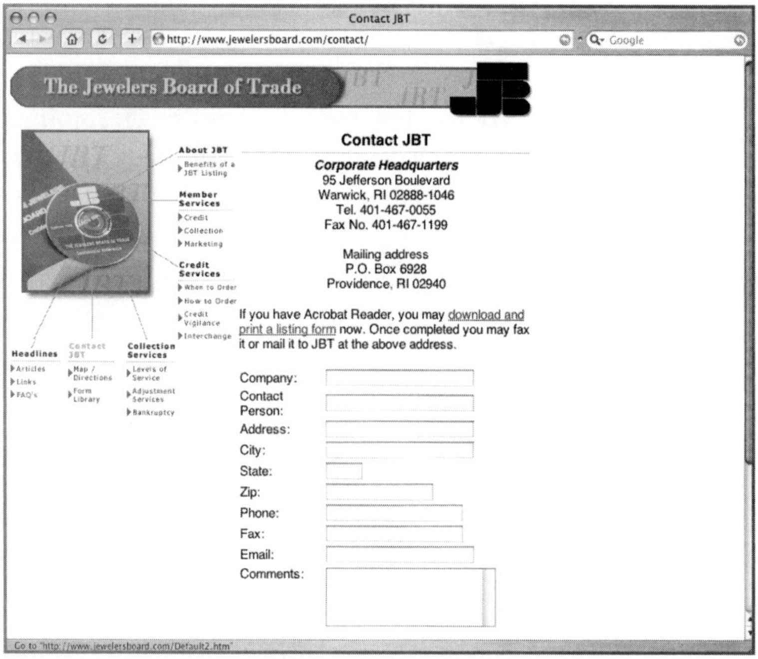

Figure 15.8

Visit the Jewelers Board of Trade Web site to download an application form.

The added bonus, and one of the true treats for Polygon members, is a well-established discussion board that Polygon members (many of whom are seasoned professionals) use to talk about anything and everything having to do with running a successful jewelry business, dealing with difficult issues, and more. You'll actually find many fellow eBay sellers here, especially the kind who use eBay to supplement a bricks-and-mortar business.

If you're accepted as a member, there is a membership fee of $90 a month. And while membership isn't a necessity (certainly not as important as a JBT number, for instance), it will help establish you as a valid member of the industry, give you to access to many different resources, and enable you to do business with a new breed of suppliers.

Visit http://www.polygon.net, shown in Figure 15.9, to find out more about applying for membership.

Figure 15.9

Polygon.net is the jewelry industry's premier online community.

Education

The most successful professional in any field is the one who's always learning. You've done your homework by familiarizing yourself with the basics, but now that you're a more advanced seller, consider getting some formal education in gemology (the study of gemstones and metals) or jewelry-making techniques. A few of the most prestigious educational institutions for jewelers have courses that you can take in your region or offer e-learning or distance learning. Here are a few recommendations:

- **Gemological Institute of America.** The GIA has been called "the Harvard of gemology"—it's the largest institution for gemology research and education. Serious jewelers attend the GIA campus to earn a two-year graduate gemologist degree, but GIA also offers distance-learning and traveling courses. To get a solid foundation, consider GIA's Essentials courses, which are available for diamonds, colored stones, cultured pearls, and finished jewelry. As a distance-learning student, you interact with instructors and other students in GIA's online Virtual Campus. As an enrolled student, you'll even get real gemstones to play with as you study. You can also take advantage of extension classes to get hands-on experience. For a complete list of available courses, visit http://www.gia.edu.

- **International Gemological Institute.** IGI is based in Antwerp, Belgium. Many industry professionals travel to Antwerp to take IGI's two-week diamond courses. For those who can't make the trip, IGI offers its Diamond Home Study Correspondence Course. Graduates receive an IGI Diamond Diploma.

- **Antique and Period Jewelry and Gemstone Conference.** Every July, the University of Maine hosts a five-day conference where participants get hands-on experience studying and working with estate jewelry. The conference is the premier opportunity to concentrate on specific periods and designers, plus network with estate jewelry experts.

Also check with your local university or community college to find out if they offer any jewelry-making classes or workshops.

In Conclusion

Becoming an expert on buying and selling jewelry on eBay will, like anything else, require some trial and error. At first, as you learn how to bid successfully and responsibly, you might feel a bit clumsy; you might struggle with the right formula for auction descriptions and sales policies; and you might even from time to time have run-ins with eBay's dark underbelly. But once you get beyond all that, shopping for jewelry and establishing a jewelry business on eBay can be incredibly rewarding—and not only from a profit standpoint. Take Kristy, whose success buying and selling jewelry on eBay allows her to stay home with her children full-time; she summed it up perfectly:

I am by no means an expert, but I *love* the jewelry I sell, and because of that, I have fun buying and selling … It never gets dull. I have made friends through eBay, and I get gifts from my buyers. There is a lot of joy in this business, if you let it come to you.

eBay opens the door to anybody who loves jewelry as much as Kristy does—the romance, the style, the sparkle, the status, and the miracle of it. You can use the information I've shared with you in this book to chart your path into this wonderful world. But your success will lie in the imagination and passion inspired by the beautiful, bejeweled treasures you trade with the other eBayers who share your love of jewelry and watches.

part 4

appendix A

Glossary

Numbers and Symbols

4Cs The four main characteristics used to determine quality in a diamond or colored gemstone: cut, clarity, color, and carat weight.

A

akoya A type of cultured pearl that originates from saltwater mollusks, usually in Japan or China; the pearls are typically white, round pearls ranging from 3 millimeters to around 9 millimeters in size.

alloy The mixture of two or more metals, usually to create a harder and more stable substance for the creation of jewelry, coins, and other objects.

antique jewelry Jewelry that is more than 100 years old.

Art Deco A style of jewelry designed circa 1920 to 1935 and characterized by geometric and symmetric shapes.

Art Nouveau A style of jewelry designed circa 1880 to 1914 and characterized by flowing, organic lines and whimsical flower, plant, and insect motifs.

Arts and Crafts A style of jewelry designed circa 1890 to 1914 that acted as transition between Art Nouveau and Art Deco, with designs that were still organic but that took on more geometrical shapes.

automatic watch A mechanical watch that winds itself as the wearer moves his arm.

B

bench jeweler A professional who specializes in designing, manufacturing, casting, and repairing jewelry.

black pearl A type of cultured pearl that originates from saltwater mollusks in the South Seas, usually French Polynesia and surrounding areas; the pearls usually have a black or gray base but feature overtones of green, pink, blue, and violet, and typically range in size from 8 millimeters to 11 millimeters.

brilliant cut A style of cutting a diamond that produces a round shape with 58 facets; often the most expensive cut for a diamond, because a round stone often weighs more than other shapes.

C

cabochon cut A gemstone cut that is rounded and polished into a dome shape rather than faceted.

carat A unit of weight used to measure the size and value of a diamond or colored gemstone; 1 carat equals 0.2 grams, or a little more than 0.007 ounces.

certificate A document issued by an independent gemological laboratory that grades a diamond on its main quality characteristics: carat weight, color, clarity, and shape; some, but not all, certificates also grade the quality of a gemstone's cut. Certificates are also sometimes available for colored gemstones, but typically only offer physical descriptions of the gemstone rather than a grade.

channel setting A style of setting gemstones in which several stones are set side by side into an indentation, or "channel," in a ring, then held in place by rims at the top and bottom of the channel.

chargeback The reversal of a payment made from a credit card or online payment service, restoring the money back to the owner of the account.

clarity The measure of the inclusions, or flaws, in a diamond or colored gemstone.

clarity enhancement A process that helps to hide flaws or inclusions in a diamond or colored gemstone; popular techniques include fracture filling, laser drilling, heating, and oiling.

color A grade that measures a diamond or colored gemstone's color; grades are based on a diamond's whiteness or a colored gemstone's hue and richness of color.

costume jewelry Jewelry that is made primarily of materials that have relatively no value, including plated metals, beads, or glass or crystal stones; however, depending on the jewelry's age, style, and design, the jewelry itself might have value.

counter An icon or graphic that appears on an auction page and tallies the number of "hits," or visits, a listing has received.

created Commonly called synthetic or lab-created, a diamond or gemstone that has been produced in a controlled laboratory environment, which simulates the conditions that are present when gemstones are formed in the earth; created gemstones have the exact same optical, physical, and chemical properties as their natural equivalents. This term is sometimes incorrectly used to describe simulants.

crown The top facets of a round brilliant diamond, between the table and the girdle.

cubic zirconia (CZ) A white, relatively valueless gemstone often used to simulate the look of diamonds.

cultured pearls Pearls that are formed by placing a bead or other irritant into mollusks to provoke the release of nacre, which coats the bead to become a pearl.

cut The way a gemstone is faceted—the number of facets and their dimensions and angles—to allow light to refract through the stone; also sometimes refers to the *shape* of a diamond or colored gemstone.

D

disclosure The process of notifying potential buyers about any enhancements made to the gemstones they're buying.

Dutch auction An auction format sometimes used to sell multiple, identical items; items are sold first to the highest bidders, and next to lower bidders on a first-come, first-served basis, at a final price that is the lowest bid from one of the winning bidders.

E

Edwardian A style of jewelry designed circa 1901 to 1915 and characterized by lacy, filigreed designs in platinum metal.

enhancements Processes used to alter or improve the appearance of a gemstone, either by disguising flaws or by changing the chemical makeup of the stone to change its color.

escrow A service that acts as an intermediary to securely hold a payment from a buyer until an item is received.

estate jewelry Jewelry that has been pre-owned.

F

facet A flat surface cut into a gemstone; most diamonds and colored gemstones are cut with many facets, sometimes several dozen.

fashion jewelry Another term for costume jewelry: jewelry that is made primarily of materials that have relatively no value, including plated metals, beads, or glass or crystal stones; however, depending on the jewelry's age, style, and design, the jewelry itself might have value.

filigree A design technique that creates open, intricate patterns in metal.

fine jewelry Jewelry that is made primarily of materials that are considered precious, including gold and platinum (and occasionally sterling silver) and precious gemstones.

finished jewelry Jewelry sold as a complete piece, with the gemstones already set in metal (as opposed to selling loose gemstones).

fixed price A type of auction in which buyers only have the option of paying a flat price for an item, rather than bidding for the item.

fracture filling A technique for hiding the flaws or inclusions in a gemstone (primarily diamonds), in which a chemical substance, such as a type of glass or resin, is used to fill any fissures that reach the surface of the gemstone; the treatment is reversible if the gemstone is later exposed to extreme heat.

G

gemology The science of identifying and evaluating gemstones.

gemstone beads Gemstones that have been rounded or faceted into spheres or oval or tube shapes, and then drilled through the middle so they can be strung.

girdle The widest part of a diamond or gemstone, with a thin band that separates the top (crown) and the bottom (pavilion).

gold A precious metal, the purest of which is 24 karats and very soft; often mixed with other metals to create alloys so the gold can be worked to create jewelry, coins, or other objects.

granulation A technique that adds tiny beads, usually gold, to the surface of a piece of jewelry; often found in designs inspired by the ancient world.

H–J

hallmark A stamp on the underside of a piece of precious metal jewelry that indicates the metal content and therefore complies with legal standards for selling precious metals.

ideal cut A diamond cut in which the angles and proportions are designed to allow the maximum amount of light to shine through the diamond's crown.

inclusion An imperfection in a diamond or gemstone, either from a mineral crystal lodged inside the stone or tiny fissures that occur inside the gemstone.

invisible setting A way of setting square-cut gemstones in a piece of jewelry that creates a checkerboard look, with stones set side-by-side with no visible prongs or bezels holding them in place; the jewelry is designed to hook the stones into place using notches made in each gemstone's girdle.

irradiation A gemstone enhancement that involves exposing gemstones and pearls to small amounts of radiation to change their atomic makeup, thereby changing their color.

K

karat The unit used to measure the purity of gold.

keyword spamming The process of attracting more traffic to an auction listing by using words in the auction title or description that are popular searches but do not actually pertain to the item for sale.

L

lab-created Sometimes known as created or synthetic, a diamond or gemstone that has been produced in a controlled laboratory environment that simulates the conditions present when gemstones are formed in the earth; lab-created gemstones have the exact same optical, physical, and chemical properties as their natural equivalents.

laser drilling An enhancement process in which lasers are used to remove inclusions in diamonds.

lampwork A process used to make patterned and intricately designed beads out of molten glass.

loupe A jeweler's magnifying glass, used to study the interiors of gemstones.

luster A sheen, sometimes described as a three-dimensional glow, on the surface of a cultured pearl that often provides a sign of the pearl's quality.

M

mechanical watch A wind-up watch.

merchant account A service, often provided by banks or other financial institutions, that allows a seller to accept and process credit cards.

metalsmith A professional who specializes in designing and creating precious-metal jewelry and other objects.

metallurgy The science of metals and alloys.

mint A term used to describe a vintage object that is in perfect condition and has never been used.

moissanite A white gemstone that has many of the same optical properties as a diamond, but that has different physical and chemical properties.

N–O

nacre The substance that makes up a pearl, produced by the mollusk from which the pearl originated; in cultured pearls, nacre is a thick outer coating but is not present throughout the entire pearl.

oiling A gemstone enhancement, mostly used with emeralds, that involves injecting oil to into a stone's fractures to hide the flaws.

online payment service A service that protects buyers' privacy and safety by accepting payments from a buyer's credit card or checking account, then transferring funds to the payee's account.

P

pavé A style that involves setting many tiny diamonds or gemstones side-by-side all over the surface of a piece of jewelry, to create a sparkly look.

pavilion The bottom part of a diamond or gemstone.

phishing An e-mail scam in which an e-mail appearing to be from a legitimate institution requests that the recipient click a link and enter account or other personal information; the link often appears to point to the institution's Web site but actually directs recipients to a different server altogether.

plating The process of overlaying a precious metal on top of nonprecious metal, for an expensive look at a lower price.

platinum A strong, heavy, lustrous white metal that is very rare and expensive.

polished A gemstone that has been cut and buffed to create a smooth, mirror-like, finished look.

point A unit of measurement for a diamond or gemstone; 100 points equals 1 carat.

precious gemstones A term historically used—though somewhat out of favor these days—to describe sapphires, emeralds, and rubies, the three most highly valued colored gemstones.

precious metals Gold, silver, and platinum, the three most valuable metals, as well as the metals whose sales are closely regulated by law.

princess cut A square cut used for diamonds that creates an exceptional amount of brilliance.

proxy bidding The standard style of bidding on an auction, in which a buyer enters the maximum amount she is willing to pay and allows the online auction system to place bids on her behalf up to that amount.

Q–R

quartz watch A battery-powered watch with a tiny quartz crystal that keeps time extremely accurately.

radiant cut A rectangular-shaped gemstone cut with clipped corners.

reproduction Jewelry that has been designed in the style of vintage or antique jewelry but that is actually brand new.

reserve A price threshold, not revealed to auction bidders, below which a seller will not sell an item.

Retro A style of jewelry designed circa 1940s and characterized by big, bold styles; very large gemstones; and the use of yellow and rose gold.

rough A gemstone that has not been cut or polished, and so appears as a rock-like crystal.

round brilliant cut The most popular diamond cut, which creates the most light refraction and sparkle compared to any other diamond cut.

S

semi-precious gemstones Historically, a term used for all colored gemstones beyond rubies, emeralds, and sapphires, but a term that has recently gone out of favor as other gemstones have increased in value and popularity.

shill bidding The process of bidding on one's own auction to drive up the price.

simulated gemstones Colored crystals or glass cut and polished to look like gemstones for costume jewelry. Sometimes called *simulants*.

sniping Placing a last-second bid for an auction item in order to beat out the competition.

solitaire A single gemstone set in a piece of jewelry—often a term describing rings, but also used for necklaces.

South Sea pearls Cultured pearls that originate from Australia, Indonesia, the Philippines, and surrounding areas; they often come in white, ivory, or golden colors and range in size from around 10 millimeters to as large as 20 millimeters.

spam An unwanted e-mail from an unknown sender, usually advertising a product.

sterling silver A silver alloy that is made up of at least 92.5 percent silver.

synthetic A diamond or gemstone that has been produced in a controlled laboratory environment that simulates the conditions present when gemstones are formed in the earth; synthetic gemstones (also called lab-created) have the exact same optical, physical, and chemical properties as their natural equivalents.

T

table The flat surface on top of a cut diamond or gemstone.

tension setting A jewelry setting in which the tension in a piece of metal acts as a spring to hold the gemstone in place.

U–V

underkarating The practice of selling precious metal jewelry that is stamped with the legally required hallmarks but is actually of lesser quality than the stamp indicates.

Victorian A style of jewelry designed circa 1837 to 1900, characterized by romantic styles and religious motifs.

vintage Jewelry that is at least 20 years old; this term is most often applied to collectible costume jewelry, while "estate" jewelry is more often used for fine jewelry.

W

windowed The phenomenon of being able to see directly through a gemstone from the top to the bottom due to poorly cut angles on the gemstone's pavilion.

wire transfer A service that transmits funds directly from the payer's bank account into the payee's.

Index